BENDING THE BOW

BOOKS BY ROBERT DUNCAN
from New Directions

BENDING THE BOW

Robert DUNCAN

NEW DIRECTIONS

1968

Library of Congress Catalog Card No. 68-15879
ISBN: 978-0-8112-0033-2

ACKNOWLEDGMENT: Some of the poems in this book
were first published in the following magazines:
*Audit, The Nation, Niagara Frontier Review, Open
Space, The Paris Review, Poetry* (Chicago), *The Rivoli
Review, Something, Synapse, Trobar,* and *The Yale
Literary Magazine;* in the broadsides *Wine,* and *Up
Rising,* published by Oyez; and in the books *Of The
War* (Oyez) and *Six Prose Pieces* (Perishable Press).

Text set in Aldus type by J. S. Brooke
First published clothbound and as New Directions
Paperbook 255 in 1968.

Manufactured in the United States of America
(Published simultaneously in Canada
by Penguin Books Canada Limited.)

New Directions Books are published for James Laughlin
by New Directions Publishing Corporation
80 Eighth Avenue, New York, NY 10011

EIGHTH PRINTING

CONTENTS

INTRODUCTION

THE WAR

We enter again and again the last days of our own history, for everywhere living productive forms in the evolution of forms fail, weaken, or grow monstrous, destroying the terms of their existence. We do not mean an empire; a war then, as if to hold all China or the ancient sea at bay, breaks out at a boundary we name *ours*. It is a boundary beyond our understanding. Now, where other nations before us have flounderd, we flounder. To defend a form that our very defense corrupts. We cannot rid ourselves of the form to which we now belong. And in this drama of our own desperation we are drawn into a foreign desperation. For our defense has invaded an area of our selves that troubled us. Cities laid waste, villages destroyd, men, women and children hunted down in their fields, forests poisond, herds of elephants screaming under our fire — it is all so distant from us we hear only what we imagine, making up what we surely are doing. When in moments of vision I see back of the photographt details and the daily body counts actual bodies in agony and hear — what I hear now is the desolate bellowing of some ox in a ditch — madness starts up in me. The pulse of this sentence beats before and beyond all proper bounds and we no longer inhabit what we thought properly our own.

A boy raised in Iowa has only this nightmare, crawling forward slowly, this defeat of all deep dwelling in our common humanity, this bitter throwing forth of a wall of men moving, in which his soul must dare tender awakening or close hard as an oak-gall within him. Only this terrible wounded area in which to have his soul-life. He turns from us, my very words turn from their music to seek his deaf ears in me. All my common animal being comes to the ox in his panic and, driven by this speech, we

i

sense,
gen. structure
break down

imagine only man, *homo faber*, has, comes into a speech words
mean to come so deep that the amoeba is my brother poet.

If the soul is the life-shape of the body, great stars, that are
born and have their histories we read in the skies and will die,
are souls. And this poetry, the ever forming of bodies in lan-
guage in which breath moves, is a field of ensouling. Each line,
intensely, a soul thing, a contribution; a locality of the living.

THE READERS

Standing before the advancing line of men on guard, it seemd
futile at first to speak to them. They were under a command that
meant to overcome us or to terrify us, a force aroused in the
refusal to give even the beginnings of a hearing. This is the na-
ture of all dying orders, a death so strong we are deadend to the
life-lines. Encircled, it seems as if only we few standing here had
life still striving in us. We must begin where we are. Our own
configuration entering and belonging to a configuration being
born of what "we" means.

The doctor kneeling upon the earth before me bore the full
shock of the hostile readers. No . . . Looking up, I saw the read-
ers themselves bore the shock of what they were to encounter.
Their commanders are possesst by rage, confronted by the ques- *who?*
tion we raise in the heart of things, they move their men as if
they were ranks of that rage down upon us to break that heart
or to beat from its beats gouts of life-blood until the truth of
what we mean to do, the faltering truth, dies and is done. We
drop a silent *e* from an unpronounced syllable, daring no more
than men in the seventeenth century presumed. Out of order,
we can no longer move them to consider that our liberties are
obediences of another order that moved us. We ourselves are the
boundaries they have made against their humanity.

"Look into their eyes," the doctor's wife tells me. To my right,
the onlookers call out, the soldiers are kicking the body of a
woman who is everything they despise: they kick her rich
clothes; they kick her cultured tone — they can see it in the way

she lies at their feet; they kick her meekness that, courageous to lie there affronts their victorious movement forward. "I am all right," she calls back to us.

Two of the faces I find immoveable with hatred for what I am. What have they been told I am? But the third wavers in the commanding panic and pleads with his eyes, Retreat, retreat, do not make me have to encounter you.

The Monsignor had just finisht his address to the men on guard, speaking to them of the state of their souls in this war, and I was to speak. I had stept forward to speak, when the men were orderd to march upon us and force us to retract our stand, and we, under our own orders, moved each to sit or lie upon the ground, to hold the ground of our testimony stubbornly, the individual volition of a non-violent action. It was like the presence of the poet's intent in the hearts of the people of a poem, we meant to fulfill our humanity. But we were, in turn, members of a company of men, moving forward, violently, to overcome in themselves the little company of others kneeling and striving to speak to them, a refusal of all common speech that strove to maintain itself before us.

What would I have tried to tell them? That we were unarmd? That we were not the enemy, but men of their kind? In the face of an overwhelming audience waiting for me to dare move them, I would speak to those alike in soul, I know not who or where they are. But I have only the language of our commonness, alive with them as well as me, the speech of the audience in its refusal in which I would come into that confidence. The poem in which my heart beats speaks like to unlike, kind to unkind. The line of the poem itself confronts me where I must volunteer my love, and I saw, long before this war, wrath move in the music that troubles me.

EQUILIBRATIONS

I'd like to leave somewhere in this book the statement that the real "we" is the company of the living, of all the forms Life

Itself, the primal wave of it, writing itself out in evolution, pro-
poses. Needs, as our poetry does, all the variety of what poets
have projected poetry to be.

"They" can be differentiated into "he" and "she". "We" is
made up of "I"'s, pronounced "eyes", as Zukofsky reminds us,
and "you", in whom the word "thee" has been hidden away.

Where "he" becomes "He" and "she", "She", a second power
of person comes into play. As the lastness and firstness of every
phrase is a second power.

Pound sought coherence in *The Cantos* and comes in Canto
116 to lament "*and I cannot make it cohere*". But the "*SPLEN-
DOUR , IT ALL COHERES*" of the poet's Herakles in *The
Women of Trachis* is a key or recognition of a double meaning
that turns in the lock of the Nessus shirt.

Hermes, god of poets and thieves, lock-picker then, invented
the bow and the lyre to confound Apollo, god of poetry. "*They
do not apprehend how being at variance it agrees with itself*,"
Heraklitus observes: "*there is a connexion working in both
directions.*"   *title?*

The part in its fitting does not lock but unlocks; what was
closed is opend. Once, in the scale of Mozart, a tone on the piano
key-board could be discordant; then, in Schönberg's scale, the
configuration uses all the keys, only the tone row is set. But the
harmony, the method of stringing, in which conflicts are trans-
formd in their being taken as contrasts, I mean to take in the
largesse of meanings. It is in the movement of the particles of
meaning before ideas that our ratios arise. In the confrontation,
had we danced, taking the advance of the soldiers by the number
in ranks into the choreography of the day, or, members of the
dance, sat where we were, tensing the strings between the horns
for the music's sake, the event the poem seeks might have
emerged. The poet of the event senses the play of its moralities
belongs to the configuration he cannot see but feels in terms of
fittings that fix and fittings that release the design out of itself
as he works to bring the necessary image to sight. Had the blue
of the sky and the delite eyes have in trees been preserved in the
battle; had the lives of the victims been preserved in the victory,

as the notes of the song come alive in its tune . . . Life demands sight, and writes at the boundaries of light and dark, black upon white, then color in which the universe appears, chemical information in which Argus eyes of the poem strive. War now is a monstrosity in the hands of militarists who have taken no deep thought of the art of war and its nature.

Working in words I am an escapist; as if I could step out of my clothes and move naked as the wind in a world of words. But I want every part of the actual world involved in my escape. I bring the laws that bound me into an aerial structure in which they are unbound as outlines of a prison unfolding.

The ground is compounded of negative and positive areas in which we see shapes defined. In the immediate work, puns appear. The line of the poem is articulated into phrases so that phases of its happening resonate where they will. Or lines stand as stanzas in themselves of our intention. The sentence remains. But related to a multitude of laws.

Two sonnets belonging to a series of five belong in turn to the larger configuration of the book, and their content, that concludes at this point the series, initiates a theme of Love that moves in other poems. Passages of a poem larger than the book in which they appear follow a sentence read out of Julian. I number the first to come *one*, but they belong to a series that extends in an area larger than my work in them. I enter the poem as I entered my own life, moving between an initiation and a terminus I cannot name.

This is not a field of the irrational; but a field of ratios in which events appear in language. Our science presumes that the universe is faithful to itself: this is its ultimate rationality. And we had begun to see that language is faithful to itself. Wherever we learned to read, the seemingly irrational yielded meaning to our reason. But here *language* does not mean what the tongue sounds and no more. A sign is written on the wall. The blind and deaf may read a language in shapes felt and forces inscribed. Let crowds or clouds enter at this stage; they tell us something. Olson in *Maximus*, "Letter, May 2, 1959", paces off boundary lines; and yet a poet has told me this ceases to be proper to

poetry. But surely, everywhere, from whatever poem, choreo-
graphies extend into actual space. In my imagination I go
through the steps the poet takes so that the area of a township
appears in my reading; were I to go to the place and enact the
text, I would come into another dimension of the poetry in which
Gloucester would speak to me. I am talking here about the fact
that if a man set his heart against falling in love, he will find the
poetry of falling in love empty and vain. Must I reiterate the
fact that the boundary lines in the poem belong to the poem and
not to the town?

   The poem is not a stream of consciousness, but an area of
composition in which I work with whatever comes into it. Only
words come into it. Sounds and ideas. The tone leading of *& images*
vowels, the various percussions of consonants. The play of num-
bers in stresses and syllables. In which meanings and ideas,
themes and things seen, arise. So that there is not only a melody
of sounds but of images. Rimes, the reiteration of formations in
the design, even puns, lead into complexities of the field. But
now the poet works with a sense of parts fitting in relation to a
design that is larger than the poem. The commune of Poetry
becomes so real that he sounds each particle in relation to parts
of a great story that he knows will never be completed. A word
has the weight of an actual stone in his hand. The tone of a
vowel has the color of a wing. "Dont mess up the perception of
one sense by trying to define it in terms of another," Pound
warnd. But we reflect that the ear is the organ not only of hear-
ing but of our equilibrations.

IT

Where you are *he* or I am *he*, the trouble of an Eros shakes the ⋆
household in which we work to contain our feeling in our ex-
tending our feeling into time and space. The nearness of this
shaking — it is our own actual city built as it is high on the
ground of a history written in earthquakes — makes for an
almost womanish tenderness in orders we are fierce to keep.

A girlish possibility embarrasses the masculinity of the reader. As if in all that play between Hermes and Apollo, that comedy of the thefts and infantile deceptions and seductions in which the instruments of an art came into poetry, a drama of recognitions and the domestication of recognitions took place. The primal Eros drawing the lines of attention beyond war into music where the flint strikes fire from the rock. But in the affections of familiar sentiments the blaze of the sun itself warms. Or, today, sending the currents burning in an arc, a lyre strung in an hermetic globe, we switch the deuce from *off* to *on* and sit about the table talking.

In the poem this very lighted room is dark, and the dark alight with love's intentions. *It* is striving to come into existence in these things, or, all striving to come into existence is It — in this realm of men's languages a poetry of all poetries, *grand collage*, I name It, having only the immediate event of words to speak for It. In the room we, aware or unaware, are the event of ourselves in It. The gnostics and magicians claim to know or would know Its real nature, which they believe to be miswritten or cryptically written in the text of the actual world. But Williams is right in his *no ideas but in things;* for It has only the actual universe in which to realize Itself. We ourselves in our actuality, as the poem in its actuality, its thingness, are facts, factors, in which It makes Itself real. Having only these actual words, these actual imaginations that come to us as we work.

This configuration of It in travail: giving birth to Its Self, the Creator, in Its seeking to make real — the dance of the particles in which stars, cells and sentences form; the evolving and changing species and individualizations of the Life code, even the persons and works of Man; giving birth within Its Creation to the Trinity of Persons we creatures know, within which in the Son, "He", is born and dies, to rise as the morning forever announces, the Created Self, Who proclaims the Father, first known as He named Himself to be Wrath, Fiery Vengence and Jealousy, to be made or revealed anew as Love, the lasting reason and intent of What Is — this deepest myth of what is happening in Poetry moves us as it moves words. The moralist must always be outraged by what God finds good; for God works, as the creative artist works, not with a sense of rewards and punishments, but to fulfill the law that he creates. He seeks in His Creation intensifications of Its orders. In the plenitude of His powers, He works always upon the edge of arbitrary alternatives; He could, we know, change the work if He would. But first among His powers is His Oneness in creation: the universe is faithful to itself. So, too, the poet has every freedom that keeps alive within itself this faithfulness to the poetry he creates. *poet || God*

Back of my person, my creaturely being, as words shift from words of my mouth, expressing, to words of the poem, creating, Man His-Her-Self, my immediate Creator, moves — the poet, His-Her agent — and would force me to some agony of my resources I dare not come to sufficient for the birth of the Created Self. In this figure, my own breath becomes a second, the breath of the poem. Olson's "the breathing of the man who writes" made anew in the breath of the line. But there is the third: the inspiration, the breath of Creation, Spiritus Sanctus, moving between the creator breathing and the breath of his creature. ★ Q

Had all the old orders passed from belief into the imagination that Hesiod could *write* a theogony? The real universe of Christendom had so become an imaginary world by the thirteenth century that Dante could enter it in a poem as primary vision and explore even its mysteries in the structure of his rimes. And kings in Shakespeare had become play kings, dramatis personae. Now, as the cry *God is dead!* out of Romantic poetry deepens the crisis of Protestant theologies a hundred years later, in poetry God is resurrected. All this making of universes in language becomes resonant with the living reality of His passion. Father Son and Spirit, with the saints and the Virgin, Mother of God, become authorities of the Imagination in which Logos is Beginning. The persons of It have revealed themselves in Eternity as the authors of the gods. From the seed of first light the galaxies move out to the extremities of imagined time and space; Lucifer "falling" is the circumference or boundary of the need for Creation.

ARTICULATIONS

The artist, after Dante's poetics, works with all parts of the poem as *polysemous*, taking each thing of the composition as generative of meaning, a response to and a contribution to the building form. The old doctrine of correspondences is enlarged and furtherd in a new process of responses, parts belonging to the architecture not only by the fittings — the concords and contrasts in chronological sequence, as in a jigsaw puzzle — by what comes one after another as we read, but by the resonances in the time of the whole in the reader's mind, each part as it is conceived as a member of every other part, having, as in a mobile, an interchange of roles, by the creation of forms within forms as we remember.

But this putting together and rendering anew operates in our apprehension of emerging articulations of time. Every particular is an immediate happening of meaning at large; every present activity in the poem redistributes future as well as past events. This is a presence extended in a time we create as we keep words in mind.

The immediate event — the phrase within its line, the adjoining pulse in silence, the new phrase — each part is a thing in itself; the junctures not binding but freeing the elements of configuration so that they participate in more than one figure. A sign appears —" . " — a beat syncopating the time at rest; as if there were a stress in silence. He strives not for a disintegration of syntax but for a complication within syntax, overlapping structures, so that words are freed, having bounds out of bound.

So, the artist of abundancies delites in puns, interlocking and separating figures, plays of things missing or things appearing "out of order" that remind us that all orders have their justification finally in an order of orders only our faith as we work addresses. Were all in harmony to our ears, we would dwell in the dreadful smugness in which our mere human rationality relegates what it cannot cope with to the "irrational", as if the totality of creation were without ratios. Praise then the interruption of our composure, the image that comes to fit we cannot account for, the juncture in the music that appears discordant.

In a blast, the poem announces the Satanic person of a president whose lies and connivings have manoeuvred the nation into the pit of an evil war. What does it mean? It is a mere political event of the day, yet it comes reveald as an eternal sentence. Polysemous — not only the nation but the soul and the poem are involved in the event. In these days again the last day, the final judgment, in a form that knows only what the here and now knows of first days or last days. What is out of joint with the times moves as this poetry moves towards a doubling of the joint in time, until, multiphasic, we would imagine the figure we had not seen in which the joining is clear where we are.

For these discords, these imperatives of the poem that exceed our proprieties, these interferences — as if the real voice of the poet might render unrecognizable to our sympathies the voice we wanted to be real, these even artful, willful or, it seems to us, affected, psychopathologies of daily life, touch upon the living center where there is no composure but a life-spring of dissatisfaction in all orders from which the restless ordering of our poetry comes.

OCTOBER-NOVEMBER 1967
—SAN FRANCISCO

BENDING THE BOW

He's given me his *thee* to keep,
secret, alone, in Love's name,
for what sake I have only in faith.

Where it is . . . ? How it is near . . . ?
I would recognize him by the way he walks.
But it was so long ago and I was never sure   •

except in his regard and then
sure as the rose scattering its petals to prepare is sure
for the ripeness near to the perfection of the rose.

I would know the red *thee* of the enclosure
where thought too curls about, opens
out from, what's hid,

until it falls away, all the profuse allusion let go,
the rose-hip persistence of the truth hid therein from me

enduring.

Sounding the triangle he rings notes the eye signs, signatures of seeing in what is seen. In the grand collage signs flash green against blue, black against white, red against yellow. Enlarged pupils of the emerging doctrine attend the hidden teacher of the increasing sound.

And all the signs rime. When you turn up the time into the rock-and-roll frenzy, the old bacchanal wave of noontide over noontide is there. The pull-blinds sing in the light. The voices of devout shouters fill the car as it goes.

So we leap forward into the ballad, the USA, high way • leads us on, feeds us • children of Orpheus where the Black Aces, the Four Corners, the Hot Stars, turn on. The sun a red ball no longer of light but of the down dipping heat of the day comes at the horizon. As if ready to go out for us.

Enters the triangle where the eye turns on to the rays of sound upon sound. But the ideogram is of silence. The roaring wave follows the line of the woman's arm, to rest in her hands, poised where they cross, crossing and signing her thighs, her zone.

5th SONNET

Love too delighting in His numbers
keeps time so that our feet
dance to be true to the count,
repeating the hesitation, the

slight bow to His will in each change,
the giving up, His syncopation,
the receiving   an other
measure again.

       You were not there,
but in love with you I danced
this round, my feet
willingly sped to its numbers,

my glance wed to the glance exchanged,
      for the design's sake,
in Love's calling. As if
in the exchange of lives,

that music that most moves us,
unknowing and true to what
I do not know, where other
lovers in intermingling figures

come and go, there were a constant
First Caller of the Dance
Who moves me, First Partner, He
      in Whom
you are most you.

SUCH IS THE SICKNESS OF MANY A GOOD THING

Was he then Adam of the Burning Way?
hid away in the heat like wrath
    conceald in Love's face,
or the seed, Eris in Eros,
    key and lock
of what I was?   I could not speak
    the releasing
word.   For into a dark
    matter he came
and askt me to say what
    I could not say.   "I . ."

All the flame in me stopt
    against my tongue.
My heart was a stone, a dumb
    unmanageable thing in me,
a darkness that stood athwart
    his need
for the enlightening, the
    "I love you" that has
only this one quick in time,
    this one start
when its moment is true.

Such is the sickness of many a good thing
that now into my life from long ago this
refusing to say I love you has bound
the weeping, the yielding, the
    yearning to be taken again,
into a knot, a waiting, a string

so taut it taunts the song,
it resists the touch. It grows dark
to draw down the lover's hand
from its lightness to what's
    underground.

BENDING THE BOW

We've our business to attend Day's duties, *day*
bend back the bow in dreams as we may   *night*
til the end rimes in the taut string
with the sending. Reveries are rivers and flow
where the cold light gleams reflecting the window upon the
   surface of the table,
the presst-glass creamer, the pewter sugar bowl, the litter
   of coffee cups and saucers,
carnations painted growing upon whose surfaces. The whole
composition of surfaces leads into the other
             current disturbing
what I would take hold of. I'd been → *when what happened?*

in the course of a letter—I am still
in the course of a letter—to a friend,
who comes close in to my thought so that
the day is hers. My hand writing here
there shakes in the currents of . . . of air?
of an inner anticipation of . . . ?   reaching to touch
ghostly exhilarations in the thought of her.

       At the extremity of this
         design
"there is a connexion working in both directions, as in
        the bow and the lyre"—   *quoting who?*
only in that swift fulfillment of the wish   *Hermes! (intro iv)/*
       that sleep   *Heraklitus*
     can illustrate my hand
      sweeps the string.

You stand behind the where-I-am. *ref. to Euricides*
The deep tones and shadows I will call a woman.
The quick high notes . . . You are a girl there too,
   having something of sister and of wife,
        inconsolate,

7

could charm all living things & stones w/ music, tried to bring wife back from the dead

and I would play Orpheus for you again,

recall the arrow or song
to the trembling daylight.
from which it sprang.

from the Emperor Julian, *Hymn to the Mother of the Gods*:

*And Attis encircles the heavens like a tiara, and thence
sets out as though to descend to earth.*

•

*For the even is bounded, but the uneven is without bounds
and there is no way through or out of it.*

TRIBAL MEMORIES   PASSAGES 1

And to Her-Without-Bounds I send,
wherever She wanders,   by what
          campfire at evening,

among tribes setting each the City where
                we Her people are
at the end of a day's reaches   here
          the Eternal
lamps lit, here   the wavering human
          sparks of heat and light
glimmer, go out, and reappear.

For this is the company of the living
and the poet's voice speaks from no
          crevice in the ground between
               mid-earth and underworld
breathing fumes of what is deadly to know,
               news larvae in tombs
          and twists of time do feed upon,

but from the hearth stone, the lamp light,
          the heart of the matter where the

                    house is held   •

yet here, the warning light at the edge of town!

9

The City will go out in time, will go out
        into time, hiding even its embers.
And we were scatterd thruout the countries and times of man

for we took alarm in ourselves,
                rumors of the enemy
spread among the feathers of the wing that coverd us.

    •

Mnemosyne, they named her, the
            Mother with the whispering
        featherd wings.   Memory,
the great speckled bird who broods over the
            nest of souls, and her egg,
    the dream in which all things are living,
I return to, leaving my self.

I am beside myself with this
        thought of the One in the World-Egg,
enclosed,   in a shell of murmurings,

                rimed round,
                sound-chamberd child.

It's that first!   The forth-going to be
                bursts into green as the spring
            winds blow watery from the south
and the sun returns north.   He hides

        fire among words in his mouth

and comes racing out of the zone of dark and storm

                towards us.

I sleep in the afternoon, retreating from work,
reading and dropping away from the reading,
as if I were only a seed of myself,
    unawakend,   unwilling
            to sleep or wake.

A cat's purr
in the hwirr thkk   *"thgk, thkk"*
of Kirke's loom on Pound's Cantos
          "I heard a song of that kind . . ."

my mind a shuttle among
          set strings of the music
lets a weft of dream grow in the day time,
          an increment of associations,
     luminous soft threads,
the thrown glamour, crossing and recrossing,
          the twisted sinews underlying the work.

Back of the images, the few cords that bind
     meaning in the word-flow,
               the rivering web
          rises among wits and senses
gathering the wool into its full cloth.

The secret!   the secret!   It's hid
          in its showing forth.
The white cat kneads his paws
          and sheathes his eyes in ecstasy against the light,
     the light bounding from his fur as from a shield
          held high in the midst of a battle.

What does the Worm work in His cocoon?

     There was such a want in the old ways
          when craft came into our elements,
     the art shall never be free of that forge,
               that loom, that lyre—

     the fire, the images, the voice.

Why, even in the room where we are,
          reading to ourselves, or I am reading aloud,
     sounding the music,
                    the stuff

vanishes upon the air,
line after line thrown.

Let there be the clack of the shuttle flying
forward and back,   forward and
back,

warp, *wearp, varp*:   *"cast of a net, a laying of eggs"*
from **warp-   "to throw"*

the threads twisted for strength
that can be a warp of the will.

"O weaver, weaver, work no more,"
Gascoyne is quoted:
"thy warp hath done me wrong."

And the shuttle carrying the woof I find
was *skutill   "harpoon"*   —a dart, an arrow,
or a little ship,

navicula   weberschiff,

crossing and recrossing from shore to shore—

prehistoric **skutil *skut-*
"a bolt, a bar, as of a door"
"a flood-gate"   •

but the battle I saw
was on a wide plain,   for the
sake of valor,
the hand traind to the bow,
the man's frame
withstanding,   each side

facing its foe for the sake of
the alliance,
allegiance, the legion, that the
vow that makes a nation
one body not be broken.

Yet it is all, we know, a mêlée,

a medley of mistaken themes
grown dreadful and surmounting dread,

so that Achilles may have his wrath
and throw down
the heroic Hektor who raised
that reflection of the heroic

in his shield . . .

Feb. 4-11   1964

The white peacock roosting
might have been Christ,

      featherd robe of Osiris,

the radiant bird, a sword-flash,

        percht in the tree   •

and the other,   the fumed-glass slide

   —were like night and day,

the slit of an eye opening in

     time

vertical to the horizon

    •

I'd cut the warp
to weave that web

      in the air

    and here

let image perish in image,

      leave writer and reader

 up in the air

  to draw

        momentous

          inconclusions,

ropes of the first water
     returnd by a rhetoric

    the rain swells.

Statistically insignificant as a locus of creation
    I have in this   my own

      intense

    area of self creation,

             the Sun itself
insignificant among suns.

     The magi of the probable
     bring forth a mirror,   an

        iridescence,   an ocean

   which I hold in the palm of my hand   •

        as if I could cast a shadow •

    to surround •

what is boundless　•
as if I could handle　•　this pearl　•　that touches
upon every imagination of what
I am　•
wrong about the web,　　the
reflection,　　the lure of the world
I love.

so pleasing   a light
            round,   haloed,   partially
disclosed,   a ring,
            night's wedding signet   •

            may be
a great lady drawing
            her tide-skirts up   •
                        in whirls
            and loosening to the gilt
                        shore-margins   of her sea-robes

•   or he,   his consent
            releasing dreams,
            the dazzling path remaining
                        over the waves,
            a lord too,   lunar moth king
                        Oberon   •   gleaming amidst clouds.

      From what source
      the light of their faces,   the
                        light of their eyes,   the dark
      glance that illumines,   the kindling look
            as if over the shimmer of the lake
                        his flesh radiant   •

My Lord-and-Lady Moon

upon whom

as if with love

the sun at the source of light

reflects   •

Lifted   •

Mount Shasta in snowy reverie

•   floats

paste-up,   the city

we build up of blocks,   the

alpha   beta   and this γ

is gamma   so placed   *Anaïs Nin*

as Henry Miller once named the Delta △ *(Erotica)*

▽ his vehicle,   and   ~~Delta~~ *of Venus*

Her zone, Her <u>parvis</u> *enclosed area in front of*
a cathedral or church

is language Pythagoras knew,   *Sex || religion*

leading to <u>the life-door, the cunt</u>

[I mean to force up emblems again into these passages of a
poetry, passages made conglomerate, the pyramid that dense, a
mountain, immovable; cut ways in it then and <u>trick the walls</u>
<u>with images establishing space and time for more than the maker</u>
<u>knows he acknowledges, in it]</u> → *is it prose.??*

why this prose break?

<u>This way below is the way above,</u> *sex → cosmos?*
the mouth of the cave or temple growing moist   *god?*

shining,   to allow   the <u>neophyte</u> *new convert*

full entrance.

<u>The body of the poem, aroused,   having</u>

what <u>mouths?</u>

It wont smear, it can be

moved,   can move,   but

no word, it's that clear,   is

19

soft, shit, painty •   Can consonants

           so crawl or blur   to give . . .

contrive to imitate juices, excretions, the body's

           spit?

      beyond how wet the air will

      come and carry these vowels?

          these dentals, labials, the tongue

so adamantly insists upon?

         this rrrr .   to be a river

      and I place here, my air;

      this block with

           for elefant

       is throne,   is soft, and

as far as I get in the play

    runs down   •

                          (4/1/64)

        runs away with me

    and I enter the wave of it.

How long have I been waiting,

       the language, the sea, the body

   rising above

     sleep

   above

        and leaves us

fallen back

20

above sleep   ·

the moon taking over tides of the mind,

pulling back
     whatever cover love had

until the <u>reefs</u> upon which we lie are exposed,

  the <u>green water</u> going out over

               the rock ledges,

body upon body

   turning keys as the <u>tide</u> turns

and reaching up into . . .

  In the curve of the dark

     the light strives

        where they come

. . . the <u>roll of the returning waters</u>
<u>over the stone stretches</u>

            remotely

reaching us.

water over stone
soft over hard

ENVOY PASSAGES 7

Good Night,   at last
the light of the sun is gone
        under Earth's rim
                and we
can see the dark   interstices
        Day's lord erases.

STRUCTURE OF RIME XXIII

Only passages of a poetry, no more. No matter how many times the cards are handled and laid out to lay out their plan of the future—a fortune—only passages of what is happening. Passages of moonlight upon a floor.

Let me give you an illusion of grieving. In the room at the clean sweep of moonlight a young man stands looking down. An agony I have spoken of overtakes him, waves of loss and return.

But he would withdraw from the telling. We cannot tell whether rage (which rimes) or grief shakes him. Let me give you an illusion of not grieving.

the ones of the old days

.

will not be done with us

but come to mind   .

thought designing for their sake

chariots and horizons   .

from which they come

towards us

ever   .

from which they come towards us,

in the distance,   nearing

where we are   I am

at the lips   before speech,   at life's

labia,   Her   crack of a door opening,

her cunt   a wound now

the gash in His side

from which monthly   blood flows   .

so Zinzendorf saw,

all maidens bear Christ's sign   with them

.   at this flowing

souls gather   .

At the babe's birth

the whole woman

opens   •   the flower bleeding,   life-lanced   •

    the head of the embryo

shoved forth from its red pod,   from the pain she knows,

      into the Child's place

      •   cries.

    "To be born again from the wound in His side"

From the horizon   ancestral

    echoes ring   •

In the streams of the wound they
*"want to have little beds, and tables,
and everything else."*

"... it must have recesses. There is a great charm in a room
broken up in plan, where that slight feeling of mystery is given
to it which arises when you cannot see the whole room from any
one place .. when there is always something around the corner"

from the window-shelter

the light

the curtains of daffodil-yellow

light

beyond •

a little night music

after   noon

• strains of *Mahagonny* on the phonograph

distant

intoxications of brazen crisis,

the (1930) *Können einem toten Mann nicht helfen* chorus

the procession with drum-roll

in the distance

recesst

(the stage becomes dark)

from the bookcases   the glimmering titles arrayd   keys

Hesiod • Heraklitus • *The Secret Books of the Egyptian Gnostics* . . .

"Take a house planned in this way, with a big living room, its great fireplace, open staircase, casement windows, built-in seats, cupboards, bookcases .. and perhaps French doors opening out upon a porch"...

La Révélation d'Hermès Trismégiste
Plutarch's Morals: Theosophical Essays
Avicenna
The Zohar
The Aurora

I was reading while the music playd

        curld up among the ornamental cushions

..."which links the house with the garden / and

    sparkling into the jeweld highlights given forth by
        copper, brass, or embroideries"

"the staircase, instead of being hidden away in a small hall or treated as a necessary evil, made one of the most beautiful and prominent features of the room because it forms a link between the social part of the house and the upper regions"...

    Below the house   in the dark of the peppertree

  stript to the moonlight   embraced

     for the mystery's sake   mounting

       thru us • the garden's recesses

"   'You are to make it,' I told you in the past. I do not suppose you recognize me. 'Owl' is what I am calld. This is how I am."

    They saw an owl.

Phantastes, At the Back of the North Wind,
    The Princess and the Goblin,
        The Princess and Curdie,   Lilith

the lamplight   warm   upon the page where I   •

romance   •   in which lost, reading   •

"   *You will often tell the story.   If you do that you*
will be able to marry those you love. You will fear
me. If I even see you, you will die."

. . ."which belong to the inner and individual part of the family life."

Willingly I'll say there's been a sweet marriage
                all the time   a ring
      (if wishing could make it so)   a meeting
            in mind   round   the moon
means rain.

                    In the beginning there was weeping,
      an inconsolable grief
                I brought   •   the storm I came in,
            the driving rain
                  the night-long
                          torrents of wind.

          Was that *that* time?   Or was it
another time   •   all the time   the torrents
          of love-making,   hiding my inconsolable grief
                in your arms.   Sometimes
when I am away from you
                    I have to make that journey,
          the journey to you   as if blindly   again
      along steps I have memorized—
                not to forget,   not to forget   •   the way
                the way you are,
            having no more weight nor strength to go by
                than my will,   my wraith,

29

calling-up the steps   •   to the house, the door, the stairs,
the hall, the room's dimensions, the

where you are

to come to you   •

my helplessness that   must somehow be a help

for you   •

Willingly I'll say there's been a sweet

marriage

and I would fill your arms

as if with flowers   with my forever

being there   •

"French doors

opening out upon a porch which
links the house with the garden."

*"There is really no circumstance of human life,
in which He has not at times been our forerunner."*

The grail broken,
the light gone from the glass,

we would make it

anew.

From the thought of the smasht gold or silver cup

once raised to lips,

we would raise *shadows* to hold the blood the drinkers

desire so • that now

my fellow poets   Blaser, Spicer, Turnbull   tell

the beads of that story again,

raise hallows   as if there were a land . . .

There was a land and a time in which we were.

Where the poem would kneel   an ake   rose in my knees,

and the poem knelt in the rosy light of the ake

so that where the cup was raised up

as if the air had lips,

in the shade of my words raised,

in the flame of my words raised,

my mind worried about the sullen ake,

the hot sun

raising a fever where I lay sweating in the room.

Was it forewarning of some disease? a
    painful core of the body's aging?   The ear
catches rime like pangs of disease from the air.   Was it
    sign of a venereal infection raging in the blood?   For poetry
    is a contagion   •   And Lust a lord
    who'll find the way to make words ake and take on
    heat and glow.

There is a land and a time—Morgan le Fay's—
    marsh and river country,   her smoky strand
in whose lewd files I too have passt   •   to
    tell the beads of that story again.

There appeard to him such a one as he hunted for,
    a beast of golden hue and antlerd crown,
led on, as it were bound by a false word, to search
    the maiden carrying the bleeding head
    commands.   Lady whose bright laughter
rings avid,   and my heart dismays   •   For I
    dread me sore to pass this forest.

The feverish youth   challenges the red man
    who throws him down,   where he is,
    (he takes his head off)
He turns aside,   face into the heat,   groaning

The while •   They brought forth

    certain wonders he did not remember what

    and among those shadows

    the shadowy cup passt.

Sick desire!   Lovesick desire!
"On vit plusieurs vies d'hommes en l'espace d'une heure."

"Commence," dit le guitariste au marbrier.

He draws the sounds forth from his drunken violin
Bacchus in delirium cuts from the stone with a saw.

What does he play?   What does he   attempt to play?
It makes no difference,   the first ayre comes,

                              and suddenly,

an energy, a melody   suave, capricious   •

       all the time   encircles me,

stifles the cry in my mouth, stops the beat
of my heart, conceals the rage of the child squalling,

                until I lie at the edge

 •   all the time, I have been   at the edge of this

          avidity, this din.   *La guitare chante.*

     He lies in wait   for the passing glance, the aroused
             glitter,   the sullen

change in the light of this   •   hard-on the music presses
                its rime   *que le violon*

ne s'entend plus   but gives itself over to the need,

        the guitar's imperative.   Release,

    I sing, without sound: Release the thunders

    from this cloud   that gathers   impending

          song.   The threatening air,

34

the drunken air,   that has broken thru,   I sing
        without sound   to take over   the

        aroused marbler.

The guitar takes over, takes the voice,
                its sound enormous,   the enormous

        sonority at the edge of the void   •

                                The voice

chatters, it chants, it declaims with a frightful verve.
(He cuts the marble with his saw   to answer)

        •   a surety   a sure thing.

The guitar   moves in   with a purity unknown to speech
improvises a variation upon the theme of the blind violin

        following his lead.

        The marble-cutter lets himself be led by him.
        He takes on splendidly and as if in marriage
        the high-pitcht nakedness of his wooing tones.

And now where is he?   What sun
        contemplates his last dreams?   What soil

    receives his cast-off skin?   What ditch
            shelters his agony?   Where are those

        thick perfumes of those lost flowers,
                        mimosas of those afternoons?

Where are the fairy colors of long-gone suns

        bedded down?

                        "Je vois longtemps
la mélancolique lessive d'ors
    du couchant."

In the joy of the new work he raises horns of sublime sound into the heat surrounding the sheets of crystalline water to make walls in the music.

And in every repeat majestic sequences of avenues branch into halls where lovers and workers, fathers, mothers and children gather, in a life, a life-work, the grand opus of their humanity, the old alchemists' dream. They must work with the first elements, they must work with the invisible, servants and students of what plants and insects say,

not of the future. This city and its people hide in the hideous city about us, among the hideous crowds in this street. Was there ever before such stupidity, such arrogance, such madness? But from these cinders the old dame who appears again in our story works transitory hints of the eternal, whose jeweld gowns, coaches, palaces, glass shoes . . .

and lights in the hearts of certain youths the unquenchable yearning for bliss, so that they know not what to do but must go as the thought of bliss sends them. So these horns pierce the blue tents above us, rending the silence because what illusions? faeries? have awakend in the Real new impossibilities of harmonic conclusions?

And we have made a station of the way to the hidden city in the rooms where we are.

STRUCTURE OF RIME XXV

The Fire Master waits always for me to recall him from a place in my heart that is burnd or is burning. He comes to my mind where, immediate to the thought of him, his rimes flicker and would blaze forth and take over.

You too are a flame then and my soul quickening in your gaze a draft upward carrying the flame of you. From this bed of a language in compression, life now is fuel, anthracite from whose hardness the years spring. In flame

                                  beings strive in the Sun's chemistry as we strive in our meat to realize images of manhood immanent we have not reacht, but leave, as if they fell from us, bright fell and fane momentary attendants,

        wild instances,   beast-headed
                                initiators

seen in glades of the fire's blazing,

    the lion's face passing into
    the man's face, flare into
        flare,

the bright tongues of two
            languages

dance in the one light.

That he wore the god head and did not worship he should have been the first to know, deriving his self from joy and even suffering that was not his, enthralld by whatever gift came in the it seemd never exhausted by his deserving or not deserving bounty of the givers. He should have straitend his ways and not taken so easily what the daemonic suggestion gave so easily, gave away to him, but, head in the honey, he would be taken in by whatever sweetness moved him or deep sounding thing or flaming that came on him in reading the green of a tree, the promise taken in a star, or the wisdom texts of Plutarch, Boehme, or, second-hand, third-hand, whatever-hand—Orpheus out of a professor's studies, for instance. And, before he composed the theogony—but this composing was a receiving, a recognizing, a seeing that it fit—having in that what authenticity?—hadn't he heard in the great passages of Charles Olson's *Maximus* re-sounding theogony? But life shakes like a drum and would discover resonances of what it loves in its own beat, the old man wetting and heating the head of the drum until it answerd the tone he sought that sought him.

And then they will dance the Waltz of the Dead, and then the Waltz of the Flowers, and then the Waltz of the Saints who have enterd the Waltz they play. Note it is built up of passages of music we heard in Mallorca, where the Church forbade dancing, they would dance even in its being forbidden. But in the thir-teenth century, before the righteous hearts hardend against the ease of Christendom, they danced *la quinte estampie real* in the cathedral, Christ the Leader of the Waltz. But He was Himself, He said, the Waltz Itself.

Charles Olson, how strangely I have alterd and used and would keep the wisdom, the man, the self I choose, after your warnings *against wisdom as such*, as if it were "solely the issue of the time of the moment of its creation, not any ultimate except what the author in his heat and that instant in its solidity yield."

The old man tunes his drum between the bowl of fire and the bowl of water, listening to the music that is about to come.

jump	stone	hand	leaf	shadow	sun
day	plash	coin	light	downstream	fish
first	loosen	under	boat	harbor	circle
old	earth	bronze	dark	wall	waver
new	smell	purl	close	wet	green
now	rise	foot	warm	hold	cool

blood   disk

horizon   flame

The day at the window
the rain at the window
the night and the star at the window

     Do you know the old language?
     I do not know the old language.

Do you know the language of the old belief?

From the wood we thought burning

our animal spirits flee,   seeking refuge wherever,

as if in Eden,   in this   panic

lion and lamb lie down,   quail

heed not the eagle in flight before the flames high

over head go.

We see at last the man-faced roe and his

gentle mate;   the wild boar too

turns a human face.   In whose visages no terror

but a philosophic sorrow shows.   The ox

is fierce with terror, his thick tongue

slavers and sticks out panting

to make the gorgoneion face.

(This is Piero di Cosimo's great painting *A Forest Fire*, dated 1490-
1500, preserved in the Ashmolean Museum at Oxford)

He inherits the *sfumato* of Leonardo da Vinci—

there is a softening of outline,   his color fuses.

A glow at the old borders makes

magic Pletho, Ficino, Pico della Mirandola prepared,

reviving in David's song,

Saul in his flaming rage heard,   music

Orpheus first playd,

chords and melodies of the spell that binds

the many in conflict in contrasts of one mind:

"For, since song and sound arise from the cognition of the mind,
and the impetus of the phantasy, and the feeling of the heart,
and, together with the air they have broken up and temperd,
strike the aerial spirit of the hearer, which is the junction of the
soul and the body, they easily move the phantasy, affect the
heart and penetrate into the deep recesses of the mind"

Di Cosimo's   featherd, furrd, leafy

boundaries where   even the Furies are birds
and blur   in higher harmonies Eumenides;
whose animals, entering a charmd field
in the light of his vision, a stillness,
have their dreamy glades and pastures.
The flames, the smoke.   The curious
sharp focus in a glow   sight
in the Anima Mundi has.

Where in the North (1500) shown in Bosch's illumination:

Hell breaks out   an opposing music.

The faces of the deluded   leer, faint, in lewd praise,
close their eyes in voluptous torment,
enthralld by fear,   avidly
following the daily news: the earthquakes, eruptions,
flaming automobiles, enraged lovers, wars against communism,
heroin addicts, police raids, race riots . . .

cut across
time

42

caught in the *lascivia animi* of this vain sound.

And we see at last the faces of evil openly

               over us,

      bestial extrusions no true animal face knows.

There are rats, snakes, toads, Boehme tells us,

         that are the Devil's creatures.   There is

a Devil's mimic of man, a Devil's chemistry.

   The Christ closes His eyes,   bearing the Cross

      as if dreaming.   Is His Kingdom

    not of this world, but a dream of the Anima Mundi,

     the World-Ensouling?

   The painter's *sfumato* gives His face.

     pastoral stillness amidst terror,   sorrow

    that has an echo in the stag's face we saw before.

   About Him, as if to drown   sweet music out,

            Satan looks forth from

men's faces:

            Eisenhower's idiot grin, Nixon's

  black jaw, the sly glare in Goldwater's eye, or

  the look of Stevenson lying in the U.N. that our

  Nation save face •

His face multiplies from the time of Roosevelt, Stalin,

  Churchill, Hitler, Mussolini; from the dream

  of Oppenheimer, Fermi, Teller, Vannevar Bush,

  brooding the nightmare formulae— to win the war! the

  inevitable • at Los Alamos

  plotting the holocaust of Hiroshima •

Teller openly for the Anti-Christ

· glints of the evil that one sees in the power of this world,

"In the North and East, swarms of dough-faces, office-vermin,
kept editors, clerks, attaches of ten thousand officers and their
parties, aware of nothing further than the drip and spoil of
politics—ignorant of principles . . . In the South, no end of blus-
terers, braggarts, windy, melodramatic, continually screaming,
in falsetto, a nuisance to These States, their own just as much as
any . . . and with the most incredible successes, having pistol'd,
bludgeoned, yelled and threatend America, these past twenty
years, into one long train of cowardly concessions, and still not
through but rather at the commencement. Their cherished secret
scheme is to dissolve the union of These States. . ."

(Whitman, 1856)

faces of Princes, Popes, Prime Usurers, Presidents,
Gang Leaders of whatever Clubs, Nations, Legions   meet

to conspire, to coerce, to cut down   ·

Now, the City, impoverisht, swollen, dreams again

the great plagues—typhus, syphilis, the black buboes

epidemics,   manias.

My name is Legion   and in every nation   I multiply.

Over those who would be Great Nations   Great Evils.

Vietnam? They are burning the woods, the brushlands, the

grassy fields razed;   their

profitable suburbs spread.

44

Pan's land, the pagan countryside, they'd
lay waste.

cool	green	waver	circle	fish	sun
hold	wet	wall	harbor	downstream	shadow
warm	close	dark	boat	light	leaf
foot	purl	bronze	under	coin	hand
rise	smell	earth	loosen	plash	stone
now	new	old	first	day	jump

For the Thing we call Moon contains

   "many mountains, many cities, many houses"

And Nature, our Mother,

     hides us, even from ourselves, there;

     showing only in changes of the Moon   •   Time

"a serpent having heads growing from him

    •   *a bull and a lion,*

        the face of a god-man in the middle,

    and he has also wings, and is calld

    ageless, Xronos, father of the ages,

      and Herakles";

     is called Eros, Phanes, χρονος ευμαρης Θεος

having the seeds of all things in his body,

    Protogonos, Erikepaios, Dionysos •

These are the Names.   Wind Child, ὑπηνεμιον

       of our Night Nature

in the Moon Egg: First-Born, Not-Yet-Born,

        Born-Where-We-Are • Golden Wings,

the unlookt for light in the *aither*

      gleaming   amidst clouds.

What does it mean that the Tritopatores, *"doorkeepers and guardians of the winds"*, carry the human Psyche to Night's invisible palace,   to the Egg

     where Eros sleeps,

the Protoegregorikos, the First Awakend?   To *waken* Him

      they carried her into   his Sleep,   the winds

disturbing the curtains at the window,   moving

       the blind, the first   tap tap,   the first count or

heart beat • the guardians of the winds (words)

      lifting her as the line lifts meaning and would

light the light,   the crack of dawn in the Egg

      Night's nature shelters   before Time.

Before Time's altars,   our Mother-Nature

      lighting the stars in order,   setting

Her night-light   in the window the Egg will be.

    The breath of the stars, moving before the stars,

       breath of great Nature,   our own,   Logos,

         that is all   milk and light •

    These things reborn within Zeus,   happening anew.

"*A dazzling light* . . *aither* . . *Eros* . . *Night*"

      where we are

The first being <u>Fairyland,</u>   the Shining Land.

Paris

[NOTE: In performing the poem, passages in bold face and in Greek letter should be written on a blackboard as they arise in the course of the dance of words and phrasings that is also the earnest mimesis of a classroom exposition, keeping in the motion of the writing as in the sound of the reading the felt beat in which the articulations of the time of the poem dance.]

SPELLING   PASSAGES 15

He did not come to the end of the corridor.

He could not see to the end of the corridor.

What came beyond he did not know.

Christos, Chronos, chord are spelld with *chi*, **X**   not
  K (*kappa*)

Xristos, Xronos, Xord

chi : "the first letter of $\chi\iota\lambda\iota o\iota,\alpha\iota,\alpha = 1000$ —Later
          "X was used either simply or with points

                ·X·

          "to call attention to anything remarkable in a passage;

          "see also

          "used as an abbreviation for $\chi\rho\eta\sigma\tau o\nu$, *useful*:
          "since a collection of passages so markt
          "might make up a Xrestomathy

          "also for **Xronos** and **Xrusos** or *Gold*."

Xaire, rejoice Xaos, the yawning abyss. Xarakter,
the mark engraved, the *intalgio* of a man.
Xaris, Xaritas   grace, favor.

I want to see the sound of the names: Kirke,   Kalypso
(*kalypsis*, a curtain or veil),   Kybele . . .

Xalkis —there being kopper nearby, malaXite
Xalkeos, of kopper, bronze, brazen   •

   •   •

OE hw /hw/   written *w h* from the 13th century.

   hwat, hwen, hweel, hwile ;   but *hwa, hwoo* becomes *hoo*

   hwite

                  SOUNDS

                        Before *slumber* was *slummer*

salm, salter   •

                  thunder was þunor
                  tapestry, tapisry

/k/   examples: kan, kind, kreep, klime, kween, skin,
            skratch, thikker, brakken, siks, kase, kure,
            kreem, klame, kwarter, skwire, konker, distinkt,
            eksamplz

A K E, the verb being of the order of *take, shake, make*

   the substantive pronounced /eit∫ / or "H", until 1700

   So Shakespeare's Beatrice, for a hauke, a horse, or a
      husband, says she is
   exceeding ill *"For the letter that begins them all"*

(Dr Johnson, ignorant of the history of the words and so
   erroneously deriving them from the Greek αχος, declared
   the verb "more gramatically written *a c h e*, the
   substantive" . .more correctly pronounced /eik/)

                  49

but *ake, ache*   like *make, match; wake, watch;*
                              break, breech;   speak, speech

a nadder, a naperon, a nompere
an ewt, "a old ainshent nobbylisk"

"For weirines on me ane slummer soft Come," Dunbar sings

And Jespersen recites:

> *She was a maid* • *the maiden kween.*
> *It is made of silk* • *a silken dress.*
> *The man is old* • *in olden days.*
> *The gold is hid* • *the hidden gold.*
> *The room is nice* • *all nicen warm.*

and quotes from Conan Doyle's *The Great Shadow:*

> "I wish your eyes would always flash like that, for
> it looks so nice and manly."

> It looks so nicen manly.

A LAMMAS TIDING

*Festival of Wheat Harvest:
1st Harvest Fest of the year
(not celebrated in US)*

[I wakend in the night with the lines *"My mother would be a falconress - And I a falcon at her wrist"* being repeated in my mind. Was the word *falconress* or *falconess?* — the troubled insistence of the lines would not let go of me, and I got up and took my notebook into the kitchen to write it out at the kitchen table. Turning to the calendar to write the date, I saw it was Lammas: 2 AM, August 1, 1964.

I rememberd then that George Stanley had told me that Saturn, my birth-planet, was brilliant in the early morning sky —"But that's between one-thirty and two," he said, "when you are fast asleep, keeping the hours you do."

And, searching out the poetic lore of what America is, I had been reading Blake's *Vision of the Daughters of Albion* these last few nights just before going to sleep. *"With what sense is it that the chicken shuns the ravenous hawk?"* I had read, and I said to myself, yes, there are bloody men, and I am not one of them but of chicken-kind, for I would never draw blood. Which goes to show one should be careful of vain self-delusions entertaind at bedtime. For now my dream would have me a hawk. And, hearing my account, Jess comments: "Especially since chickens do draw blood." Whereupon, I recall those horrible cannibalistic hens I tended at Treesbank, that needed only the first sign of blood that might be left after egg-laying to tear at each other, bloody not from hunger but from malice, like so many poets furious in their pecking order.

Vietnam

> Do I draw blood then chicken-wise
> and hide myself in a hawk's disguise?

But dreams ever betray our minds, and in the poem there is another curious displacement upward, for the bell which is actually attacht to a falcon's leg by a bewit just above the jess, in the dream becomes a set of bells sewn round the hood, a ringing of sound in the childhood of the poet's head.] *?*

51

MY MOTHER WOULD BE A FALCONRESS

will to power but not nec.
power

My mother would be a falconress,
And I, her gay falcon treading her wrist,
would fly to bring back
from the blue of the sky to her, bleeding, a prize,
where I dream in my little hood with many bells
jangling when I'd turn my head.

submission

My mother would be a falconress,
and she sends me as far as her will goes.
She lets me ride to the end of her curb
where I fall back in anguish.
I dread that she will cast me away,
for I fall, I mis-take, I fail in her mission.

delight in violence

She would bring down the little birds.
And I would bring down the little birds.
When will she let me bring down the little birds,
pierced from their flight with their necks broken,
their heads like flowers limp from the stem?

I tread my mother's wrist and would draw blood.
Behind the little hood my eyes are hooded.
I have gone back into my hooded silence,
talking to myself and dropping off to sleep.

For she has muffled my dreams in the hood she has made me,
sewn round with bells, jangling when I move.
She rides with her little falcon upon her wrist.
She uses a barb that brings me to cower.
She sends me abroad to try my wings
and I come back to her.   I would bring down
the little birds to her
I may not tear into, I must bring back perfectly.

I tear at her wrist with my beak to draw blood,
and her eye holds me, anguisht, terrifying.
She draws a limit to my flight.
Never beyond my sight, she says.

She trains me to fetch and to limit myself in fetching.
She rewards me with meat for my dinner.
But I must never eat what she sends me to bring her.

Yet it would have been beautiful, if she would have carried me,
always, in a little hood with the bells ringing,
at her wrist, and her riding
to the great falcon hunt, and me
flying up to the curb of my heart from her heart
to bring down the skylark from the blue to her feet,
straining, and then released for the flight.

My mother would be a falconress,
and I her gerfalcon, raised at her will, *largest species of falcon*
from her wrist sent flying, as if I were her own
pride, as if her pride *vs. 'gay'*
knew no limits, as if her mind
sought in me flight beyond the horizon.

Ah, but high, high in the air I flew.
And far, far beyond the curb of her will,
were the blue hills where the falcons nest.
And then I saw west to the dying sun— ★
it seemd my human soul went down in flames.

I tore at her wrist, at the hold she had for me,
until the blood ran hot and I heard her cry out,
far, far beyond the curb of her will •

to horizons of stars beyond the ringing hills of the world where
    the falcons nest
I saw, and I tore at her wrist with my savage beak.
I flew, as if sight flew from the anguish in her eye beyond her sight,
sent from my striking loose, from the cruel strike at her wrist,
striking out from the blood to be free of her.

My mother would be a falconress,
and even now, years after this,
when the wounds I left her had surely heald,
and the woman is dead,

TURNING PT

biological mother — died giving birth to him

her fierce eyes closed, and if her heart
were broken, it is stilld   •

I would be a falcon and go free.
I tread her wrist and wear the hood,
talking to myself, and would draw blood.

SAINT GRAAL   (after Verlaine)

At times, dying of the period in which we live, I sense
that my immense anguish gets drunk on hope.
In vain the shameful hour opens profound mouths.
In vain disasters without end gape beneath us
to engulf the self-indulgence of our suffering,
the blood of Christ streams down from everything.

The precious Blood flows in waves from Its altars
not yet overthrown and will go on flowing
when they will be; and when our time of evil will be such
that the strongest, giving way to mortal terror,
abase themselves to the law without honor,
from the shadow of prisons it will burst forth again.

It will run forth again from the cement walls.
It will loosen the horror that cements them.   Sweet and red
sweating-out, enduring flood of orisons,
of hard expiation and of right reason taken in protest
against the acts of betrayal and cowardice, the fires
raind down upon whatever moves in the countryside,
the death-chambers and instruments
of interrogation.
                        Torrent of love
from the God Himself Love and Sweetness,
Eternal Cup He is, we moved toward, even be it
amidst the horror of this mocking world we face,
refreshing river of fire that quenches thirst,
live source where the heart may be revived,
even of the assassin, even of the adulterer,
salvation of the fatherland, O blood, gift of love,
        that quenches life's thirst!

PARSIFAL   (after Wagner and Verlaine)

Et O ces voix d'enfants, chantant dans le coupole!
T.S. Eliot, *The Waste Land*, line 202

Parsifal has put off the boys and girls, their
    babbling song and dance, their
sexy ways.   He stands
    blond and tall,
        enhanced by the magic of his not knowing
what's going on, amidst their knowing
    inclination everywhere
towards the flesh of the virgin youth.   He glows
    untoucht, most fair,
        in all those glancing shadows that
would cast their spell
    and seduce the hero to their lights of love,
        tricks of the afternoon
and one-night stands.

Parsifal has put off Kundry, the most beautiful of all
    women, She of Subtle Heart, turnd away
        from her cool arms
and the beat of blood displayd at her throat
    that would excite the soul's
        hot deep welling up of desire
and yet quench the heat.

He has put off Hell's magic fire
    and from whose glimmering halls
        falling in ruins as he turns returnd
to the tents of light burdend with a heavy prize
    his boyish arm has won
        back from the hold of hidden things.

With the Lance that pierced the side of the Lord
    he does not know Whose Name, he knows now
only what he has to do.   He heals
    the king from his anguish, brings up

　　　　out of the dark he dared,
as if it were a ray of light, the spear
　　　won back from magic's realm, returnd
　　　　　to the king, to the very king himself
long lingering at the edge of the Father's love,
　　　the priest he is himself
　　　　　of the essential Treasure.

　　　In gold robe

Parsifal adores the glory and the symbol　　　·
—but it is a simple pure dish of crystal in which shines
　　　the Blood of the Real,

pulse of the Father's love the music raises.

And O,　　the voices of the children,

　　　singing in the dome above.

No, Verlaine, I thirst for cool water, for the
    cool of the shade tree,   I would

        drink in the green of the leafy shade,

for the sweet water that wells up from under
    the rock ledge,   the mossy shadows

the coins of light,   shaken down
            drifting, dreaming in the ever-running

stream of bright water pouring over
                rocks gleaming amidst the cold

    current, s   •   words

Sept 5:   Sweet his mouth   bitter his mouth

Sept 7:   At dawn, your breath stirs   first light

                auras of the cool line of hill-horizons

    ringing,   your eyes closed,   sweet smile

        bitter smile.   The first ones are awakening.

    You come early, à l'heure juste quand tu
        te lèves,   morning your temple,
    donnant à ton image et à ton sanctuaire
        le souffle de la vie et une grande puissance

Sept 22:   a current of air.   This late in the year

    morning gets darker.

        And at the seance night holds at day's
        table

                •

            I let sadness gather

(Sept 23)

    clear light and shadow on the moving water.

    Coming across an old photograph of him
        no recognition stirs,   his time
    that was forever has slipt away.

    The key of C minor no longer belongs to
        the song I have forgotten and will never
  sing   •   the longing, the lingering
        tune of it

          •   a heavy bough of darkness above

mirrord   depth-dark   below •

    sparks of sun-light   There must be

breaks in the first-thought-solid shade

(Sept 27:)   Then Jean Genet's *Un Chant d'Amour*
    where we witness the continual song that runs thru the walls.

 I loved all the early announcements of you, the first falling
    in love,
             the first lovers

                      (Oct 1)

    mouthing the stone thighs of the night,

  murmuring and crying out   hopeless   words of endearment.

 The soldier in a dirty corner of the war
       finding his lover,   the youth   sending roots of innocence
into the criminal ground   striking   a light that illumines
    the dark belly,   the old man   recalling

      the bird's leap upward to flight towards the heart

      from his nest of hair,   his

mimesis song makes of the dewy lips the fountain forces.

Do you not know that Egypt
is the image of Heaven?

    Under the sign of the Cross

      the spells of the Kabiri have come to an end.

The Orphic Xristos descends in the magic rite—
     the driving of the nails into his hands and feet,
  the briar crown, and, before: the sweating, stumbling
   destitute carrying of the instruments of his death
      to the place of His death

Her death he comes to   to unite   Kore and Xristmas

    •   And lifts me up to him,

  lifted me up to him,   embracing   every fear I had

   of him,   every fear   he had of me   for I

was fearful.

          Grand Mi'raj!   It is the Sun, the fiery ball

  that ascends with my heart,   breaking from his horizon

   blue in which He   rides.   Great Impersonator!

 Surrogate!   Even Day I would take   to be His

I may take thought in   but must take breath   in the air

     the green leaf   creates   in the Sun's precincts.

 Immediate Star!

As for Music—to know this is to know the order of all things
  set together in a key of diversities

    is a sweet harmony.

ASKLEPIOS: *Who then will be the men after us?*

HERMES:

The time will come when Egypt will appear to have been in vain
And men, weary of life, no longer will regard the earth
as worthy object of their love and treasure in their keeping.
Then shall this holiest land be choked with tombs and corpses.

O Egypt, Egypt, of thy immortal poems
only stories will remain—the stone images, the painted realities;
the divine words cut in stone surviving their language.
For the Eternal Ones shall return to the Dream.
And their forsaken dreamers shall all die out.

O Stream of the Nile, Great River, I speak out,
my words flowing, feeding the land of my speech, Egypt,
forever,   even when men no longer revere
first things   •

And this Vision of the Cosmos in which the Greatest Good is
will be in danger of perishing. Men will esteem it a burden.
I see they come forth, having pride in their reason, to despise it,
and no longer cherish or abide in the Mind of the Universe
Nor take manhood in the music of its many powers.

None will raise his eyes to the stars at night
Nor take thought of his life in light-years and the outer reaches
of Heaven before he was;

But the soul and all the beliefs attacht to it:
That it is immortal by nature or makes for immortality,
Will be laught at and thought nonsense.   Then Earth

   will lose her equilibrations.

   "This one a great *daimon*, intermediate
      between the divine and what perishes.

61

"By Him, the Holy Spirit, all intercourse and converse
   awake and asleep.

"His intermediate powers are many,
   and this one is Eros"

John Cage's open scales

"who will be faced with the entire field of sound"

Most beautiful!   the red-flowering eucalyptus,
  the madrone, the yew

Is he . . .

So thou wouldst smile, and take me in thine arms
The sight of London to my exiled eyes
Is as Elysium to a new-come soul

  If he be Truth
  I would dwell in the illusion of him

His hands unlocking from chambers of my male body

  such an idea in man's image

rising tides that sweep me towards him

   . . . *homosexual?*

    and at the treasure of his mouth

  pour forth my soul

    his soul commingling

I thought a Being more than vast, His body leading
  into Paradise, his eyes
    quickening a fire in me, a trembling

  hieroglyph: At the root of the neck

the clavicle, for the neck is the stem of the great artery
  upward into his head that is beautiful

    At the rise of the pectoral muscles

the nipples, for the breasts are like sleeping fountains
  of feeling in man, waiting above the beat of his heart,
  shielding the rise and fall of his breath, to be
  awakend

At the axis of his mid hriff

the navel, for in the pit of his stomach the chord from
which first he was fed has its temple

At the root of the groin

the pubic hair, for the torso is the stem in which the man
flowers forth and leads to the stamen of flesh in which
his seed rises

a wave of need and desire over   taking me

cried out my name

(This was long ago.   It was another life)

and said,

What do you want of me?

I do not know, I said.   I have fallen in love.   He
has brought me into heights and depths my heart
would fear   without him.   His look

pierces my side •   fire eyes •

I have been waiting for you, he said:
I know what you desire

you do not yet know   but through me •

And I am with you everywhere.   In your falling

I have fallen from a high place.   I have raised myself

from darkness in your   rising

wherever you are

my hand in your hand   seeking   the locks, the keys

I am there. Gathering me, you gather

your Self •

For my Other is not a woman but a man

the King upon whose bosom let me lie.

Incidents of me   the eye sees

a leaf among many leaves   turning upon the stream, the screen,

the words upon the page   flow away into   no hold I have

What did it say?

(A PASSAGE)   Kraftgänge

. . . for the stars have their kingdom in the veins of
the body which are cunning passages (and the sun
has designd the arteries)   where they drive forth
the form, shape and condition of man

(Boehme),   and from Hesiod:

They live in a place apart from men,

at the ends of the earth

along the shores of the deep roaring Ocean   their campfires

their circles of great stones   their gold crowns of hair

untoucht by sorrow

having no guilt.

And what shall we have to do with them then?

For those who love us   must be heavy with sorrow

We ourselves can know no good apart
from the good of all men

Dawn which appears and sets many men on their road

the light in the east   breaking

Having the violence of great winds, thunderous waves, Thor's
hammering fire,

the jets of blood, milk, and rain
commingling

66

in the moving picture
[*Fireworks*, Kenneth Anger, 1947]

or another face

breaking into changes of agony and submission

"One voice said, 'If you go among the Trees, the Children of the Night will change your spirit. Eat and sleep here.' The other voice said, 'Ask for the Knife.' I listened to that voice."

Aurora, Jacob Boehme; Hesiod, *Works and Days*;
Rewards and Fairies, Rudyard Kipling

"I said to my Mother in the morning, 'I go away to find a thing for my people, but I do not know whether I shall return in my own shape.' She answered, . . ."

"True," Puck said. "The Old Ones themselves cannot change men's mothers even if they would."

Story, Herself a mother of sorts

When the artichoke flowers

and the grasshopper sings in the heat

let me have a seat in the shade some rock casts,

with water and good wine.

Everyone praises a different day

but few know their nature.

Sometimes a day is a step-mother,

sometimes a mother.

"She answered, 'Whether you live or die, or are made different, I am your Mother.' "

In the assembly of the years, the tears of Tyltyl rise to his eyes where Bluebeard has constructed towers of his wrath as a palace to surround the room where the Bluebird hides. Over and over again Christmas arrives, the tree in whose branches our lives are continually kindled; and the Children set out with Fire, Water, Bread and Milk—animated Things—on a progress thru the stories of the house they live in.

From the boy's slight form the bride goes up to the closed room to open the one door she was forbidden to open. She turns the essential key of the story she seeks. In the gloom of the red chamber she spies upon the hanging corpses of life after life. From the moaning body of the boy the man he is breaks like a wrathful husband his fiery torso. From the man's sensual enclosure aging the old one survives, his head shaking, hands turning over the pages, remembers as if it did not matter   •   the bride's first breaking into the silence that surrounds him, the passages from whose doors that room and all others, the shadows in passages from room to room, blood or wine, "the Sun or Heart shining into and thru all the angelic doors"

(Night, in fancy dress, "flowing black robes, covered with mysterious stars and shot with reddish-brown reflections, veils, dark poppies, etc", addresses the Children)

> I used to *make up* dreams.

> The fire in the hearth, the water in the white pitcher, the earth in the pot where the dwarf pomegranate grows and bears its first fruit, the night air in the open window

> > are kind.

> Death by fire,   death by water.

> > Fireblast and flood,

the rending air,   the

shaking earth.

Where the tents of the Great Assembly stand,

I used to make up my

tents,   my treasuries,

my powers within powers

12/14/64

not men   but heads of the hydra

his false faces in which
authority lies

hired minds of private interests

over us

here: Kerr (behind him, heads of the Bank of America
the Tribune,
heads of usury, heads of war)

the worm's   mouthpiece   spreads

what it wishes   its own

false news : 1) that the students broke into Sproul's office,
vandalizing, creating disorder; 2) that the Free Speech
Movement has no wide support, only an irresponsible min-
ority   going on strike

Chancellor Strong,   the dragon claw

biting his bowels, his bile

raging against the lawful demand

for right reason.

In this scene   absolute authority

the great dragon himself so confronted

whose scales are men officized —ossified— conscience

no longer alive in them,

the inner law silenced,   now

they call out their cops, police law,
the club, the gun, the strong arm,
gang-law of the state,
hired sadists of installd mediocrities.

The aging Professor, translator of fashionable surrealist
revolutionaries, muttering —

*They shld not be permitted to be students; they shld
be in the army.*

Where there is no commune,

the individual volition has no ground.

Where there is no individual freedom,   the commune

is falsified.

in Blake's day   "old Nobodaddy"

in whose image, reduced in spirit
Kerr

(Stevenson, lying in the U.N. to save face)

*He swore a great & solemn Oath
To kill the people I am loth.
But if they rebel, they must go to hell:
They shall have a Priest & a passing bell.*

muttering—

*"Theyv caused all this trouble in the South.   The
responsible blacks dont want to have anything to do
with them.   Now they are making trouble here.   But
theyv been arrested and fingerprinted; we know who
they are; we know how to stop them . . ."*

71

> Farted & belch'd & cough'd
> And said, 'I love hanging & drawing & quartering
> Every bit as well as war & slaughtering . . .

(in his first campaign, Stevenson, facing the Korean abattoir:
"We will continue to pursue our peaceful purposes in Asia")

> Damn praying & singing
> Unless they will bring in
> The blood of ten thousand by fighting or swinging

3) that only some three hundred students are concernd
   about freedom of speech; only
   thirty, the hard core   [Kerr]
          but behind them
  a hidden community,   three thousand
   outside the university in this
     conspiracy for free speech

This wave will retreat and men will cease to care . . .

Each day   the last day;   each day   the

       beginning   the first word

        door of the day or law awakening we create,

  vowels sung in a field in mid-morning

       awakening the heart from its oppressions.

  Evil "referrd to the root of *up, over*"
  simulacra of law that wld over-rule
    the Law man's inner nature seeks,

72

coils about them,   not men but

    heads and armors of the worm   office is

    There being no common good, no commune,
no communion, outside the freedom of

        individual volition.

That Freedom and the Law are identical
and are the nature of Man—Paradise.

The seed I am knows only the green law of the tree into which
it sends out its roots, life and branches,

        unhinderd,   the vast universe
               showing only its boundaries we imagine.

Grant me passages from winter's way,
and in the cold let me enclose my
self in sleep.   The tree is   as if dead   each
naked twig shakes in the wind.

             Gulls come in from the sea out there

               wheel above the cold roofs

                  dark days

    the incessant rain   the ground

        waterloggd.

             It is as if I were moving towards
the wastes of water all living things remember the world to be,

        the law of me
            going under the wave.

O grievous sea!
    wide sepulcher where everything seems living!
These two combatants
    made up of fury and of wind—
the pitching to and fro that slavers, the rolling round
that fumes up—wrestling upon this funereal raft in the fog
without truce, each second tear away some fragment
of the keel or bridge in their black contest.
At times, at the zenith a cloud breaks up,
for a while ominous in crumbling, and, on the prow,

a glimmer, that trembles in the breath of the South Wind,
grows dimly, half-lighting the name: Leviathan—
then the apparition is lost in the profound waters,
everything goes out!

Leviathan!   *all the ancient world is there,*
harsh, enormous in his wild ugliness, his stupidity,
          his heaviness . . .

Leviathan!   *all the future we know is there—grandeur,*
          horror. . .

     Grand Mother of Images,   matrix
genetrix,   quickening in rays
          from the first days of the cosmos,

     turning my poet's mind in tides of
solitude, seductive reveries, fears, resolves, outrage
               yet
     having this certain specific agent I am,

          the shadow of a tree wavering and yet staying

               deep in it,

     the certain number of his days renderd uncertain,

               gathering,

animal and mammal,   drawing such milk

          from the mother of stars.

BENEFICE  the sun

on the horizon
in the West

(setting)
rises

thru the Shinto Gate

as at Stonehenge the Mid-Winter Sun

rise   a message

from the Orient   West of us

4 AM   February 7th
(my mother's birth day)

the Shining Lady
at the horizon   •

we live in the darkness in back of

her   rising

sing

from the ridge-pole.

For the Good,

il ben dello intelletto,   the good of the people,

the soul's good.

I put aside

whatever I once served of the poet, master
of enchanting words and magics,

not to disown the old mysteries, sweet
muthos   our mouth's telling   •

and I will still tell the beads, in the fearsome
street I see glimpses of   I will pray again
to those great columns of moon's light,
"Mothering angels, hold my sight steady
and I will look this time as you bid me   to see
the dirty papers, moneys, laws, orders
and corpses of people and people-shit."

From house to house the armd men go,

in Santo Domingo hired and conscripted killers
against the power of an idea, against

Gassire's lute,   the song

of Wagadu, household of the folk,

commune of communes

hidden seed in the hearts of men

and in each woman's womb   hidden.

They do not know where It is   •   at Béziers

the Abbé of Citeaux orders   *Kill them all—*

the Lord will know His own!

Pillars I saw in my dream last year, stand

in my heart and hold the blood,

my pulse rises and beats against its walls.

In the streets of Santo Domingo Herod's hosts again

to exterminate the soul of the people go

leaving behind them the dirty papers,
torn books and bodies . . .

Down this dark corridor, "this *passage*," the poet reminds me,

and now that Eliot is dead, Williams and H.D. dead,
Ezra alone of my old masters alive,   let me
acknowledge Eliot was one of them,   I was
one of his,   whose   "History has many
cunning passages, contrived corridors"

comes into the chrestomathy.

I thought to come into an open room
where in the south light of afternoon
one I was improvised
passages of changing dark and light
a music dream and passion would have playd
to illustrate concords of order in order,
a contrapuntal communion of all things   •

but Schubert is gone,
the genius of his melody
has passt, and all the lovely marrd sentiment
disownd I thought to come to, a poetry

78

having so much of beauty
that in whose progressions   rage,
grief, dismay transported— but these
are themselves transports of beauty!   The blood

streams from the bodies of his sons
to feed the voice of Gassire's lute.

The men who mean good

must rage, grieve, turn with dismay

to see how "base and unjust actions, when they are the objects
of hope, are lovely to those that vehemently admire them"

and how far men following self-interest can betray all
good of self.

There is no

good a man has in his own things except

it be in the community of every thing;

no nature he has

but in his nature hidden in the heart of the living,

in the great household.

The cosmos will not

dissolve its orders at man's evil.

"That which is corrupted is corrupted with reference to
itself but not destroyd with reference to the universe;

for it is either air or water"

Chemistry having its equations

beyond our range of inequation.

There must be a power of an ambiguous nature
and a dominion given to choice: "For the

electing soul alone is transferrd

to another and another order . . . "

effegy/superficial
likeness

Now Johnson would go up to join the great simulacra of men,
    Hitler and Stalin, to work his fame
    with planes roaring out from Guam over Asia,
all America become a sea of toiling men
    stirrd at his will, which would be a bloated thing,
    drawing from the underbelly of the nation
    such blood and dreams as swell the idiot psyche
    out of its courses into an elemental thing
    until his name stinks with burning meat and heapt honors

And men wake to see that they are used like things
    spent in a great potlatch, this Texas barbecue
        of Asia, Africa, and all the Americas,
And the professional military behind him, thinking
    to use him as they thought to use Hitler
    without losing control of their business of war,

But the mania, the ravening eagle of America
    as Lawrence saw him "bird of men that are masters,
    lifting the rabbit-blood of the myriads up into . . ."
    into something terrible, gone beyond bounds, or
As Blake saw America in figures of fire and blood raging,
    . . . in what image? the ominous roar in the air,
the omnipotent wings, the all-American boy in the cockpit
    loosing his flow of napalm, below in the jungles
    "any life at all or sign of life" his target, drawing now
        not with crayons in his secret room
the burning of homes and the torture of mothers and fathers and
  children,
    their hair a-flame, screaming in agony, but
in the line of duty, for the might and enduring fame
    of Johnson, for the victory of American will over its victims,
    releasing his store of destruction over the enemy,
in terror and hatred of all communal things, of communion,
    of communism   .

poets, children

has raised from the private rooms of small-town bosses and business-
   men,
from the council chambers of the gangs that run the great cities,
      swollen with the votes of millions,
from the fearful hearts of good people in the suburbs turning the
      savory meat over the charcoal burners and heaping their barbecue
      plates with more than they can eat,
from the closed meeting-rooms of regents of universities and sessions
      of profiteers

—back of the scene: the atomic stockpile; the vials of synthesized
      diseases eager biologists have develupt over half a century dreaming
      of the bodies of mothers and fathers and children and hated rivals
      swollen with new plagues, measles grown enormous, influenzas
      perfected; and the gasses of despair, confusion of the senses, mania,
      inducing terror of the universe, coma, existential wounds, that
      chemists we have met at cocktail parties, passt daily and with a
      happy "Good Day" on the way to classes or work, have workt to
      make war too terrible for men to wage—

raised this secret entity of America's hatred of Europe, of Africa, of
      Asia,
the deep hatred for the old world that had driven generations of
      America out of itself,
and for the alien world, the new world about him, that might have
      been Paradise
but was before his eyes already cleard back in a holocaust of burning
      Indians, trees and grasslands,
reduced to his real estate, his projects of exploitation and profitable
      wastes,

this specter that in the beginning Adams and Jefferson feard and knew
would corrupt the very body of the nation
      and all our sense of our common humanity,
this black bile of old evils arisen anew,
takes over the vanity of Johnson;
and the very glint of Satan's eyes from the pit of the hell of

America's unacknowledged, unrepented crimes that I saw in
Goldwater's eyes
now shines from the eyes of the President
in the swollen head of the nation.

EL DESDICHADO   (THE DISINHERITED)

I am the dark one, - the widower, - the unconsoled,
The prince of Aquitaine at his stricken tower:
My sole *star* is dead, - and my constellated lute
Bears the black *sun* of the *Melencolia*.

In the night of the tomb, you who consoled me,
Give me back Mount Posilipo and the Italian sea,
The *flower* which pleased so my desolate heart,
And the trellis where the grape vine unites with the rose.

Am I Amor or Phoebus? . . . Lusignan or Biron?
My forehead is still red from the kiss of the queen;
I have dreamd in the grotto where the mermaid swims . . .

And two times victorious I have crosst the Acheron:
Modulating turn by turn on the lyre of Orpheus
The sighs of the saint and the cries of the fay.

MYRTHO

I think of thee, Myrtho, divine enchantress,
Of lofty Posilipo with a thousand fires glittering,
Of thy forehead flooded with lights of the Orient,
Of the black grapes mingled with the gold of your hair.

It is in your cup too that I used to drink drunkenness,
And in the furtive lightning of your eye smiling
When I was seen praying at the feet of Iacchus,
For the Muse had made me one of the sons of Greece.

I know why the volcano has reopend over there . . .
It's because you toucht it yesterday with a light foot,
And suddenly the horizon is hidden with ashes.

Since a Norman duke broke your gods of clay,
Always, under the laurel boughs of Virgil
The pale hydrangea joins the green myrtle!

HORUS

The god Kneph in his trembling shook the universe:
Isis, the mother, then rose on her child-bed,
Made a gesture of hatred toward her savage mate,
And the ardor of the old days shone in her green eyes.

"Look at him," she said: "he dies, the old pervert!
All the frosts of the world have passt thru his mouth.
Bind his crookt foot, put out his crosst eye,
He is the god of volcanoes and the king of winters!

"The eagle has already passt, the new spirit calls me,
I have reclothed myself for him in the robe of Kybele . . .
He is the child beloved of Hermes and Osiris!"

The goddess had fled away upon her shell of gold,
The sea gave us back her adored image,
And the skies were radiant under the scarf of Iris.

ANTEROS

You ask why I have so much rage at heart
And upon a neck that could bend an unbowd head;
It's because I came from the race of Antaeus,
That I return the darts against the victorious god.

Yes, I am one of those whom the Avenger inspires,
He has markt my forehead with his inflamed lip,
Under the pallor of Abel, alas! staind with blood,
I have at times the irreconcilable blush of Cain.

Jehovah!   the last one, vanquisht by your genie,
Who from the pit of hell cried out: "O tyranny!"
That was my grandfather Belus or my father Dagon . . .

86

Three times they dipt me in the waters of Cocytus,
And, all alone protecting my mother the Amalekite,
I resow at her feet the teeth of the old dragon.

DELPHICA

Do you know, Daphne, that song of the old days,
At the foot of the sycamore or under the white laurels,
Under the olive trees, the myrtle, or the trembling willows,
That song of love that always begins again? . . .

Do you still know the TEMPLE with its immense peristyle,
And the bitter lemons where your teeth presst their mark,
And the grotto, fatal to imprudent visitors,
Where the ancient seed of the vanquisht dragon sleeps? . . .

They will return, those Gods that you always weep for!
Time is going to bring back the order of the old days;
The earth has shudderd with a prophetic breath. . . .

Meanwhile, the sibyl with the latin visage
Is still asleep beneath the Arch of Constantine
—And nothing has disturbd the severe portico.

ARTEMIS

The Thirteenth returns ... It is again She, the first one;
And She is always the One Alone,—or this is the only moment;
For art thou queen, O thou! the first or last?
Art thou king, thou the only or the last lover? ...

Love who loved you from the cradle to the grave;
She that I loved alone loves me still tenderly:
She is Death - or the Dead One ... O delite! O torment!
The rose that she holds is the *Rose hollyhock*.

Neapolitan saint with hands full of fires,
Rose violet at the heart, flower of Saint Gudule:
Didst thou find thy cross in the desert of the skies?

White roses, fall! you insult our gods.
Fall, white phantoms, from your sky that burns:
—The saint of the abyss is more saintly to my eyes!

THE CHRIST IN THE OLIVE GROVE

> *"God is dead!   the sky is empty . . .*
> *"Weep!   children, you no longer have a father!"*
> —Jean Paul Richter

I

When the Lord, lifting to the sky his thin arms,
Under the sacred trees, as poets do,
Had been for a long time lost in his mute sorrows,
And believed himself betrayd by ungrateful friends;

He turnd towards those who waited for him below
Dreaming of being kings, sages, prophets . . .
But dull with it, lost in the beasts' sleep,
And he began to cry out: "No, God does not exist!"

They slept.   "Friends, do you know the *tidings?*
I have toucht my forehead to the eternal vault;
I am broken, bloody, too long suffering!

"Brothers, I deceived you: Abyss!   abyss!   abyss!
The god is missing from the altar where I am the victim . . .
There is no God!   God no longer exists!"   But they still slept . . .

II

He began again: "Everything is dead!   I have searcht the worlds;
And I have lost my flight in their milky ways,
As far as life, in its prolific veins,
Pours out the golden sands and floods of silver.

"Everywhere, the desert soil borderd by waves,
Confused whirlpools of disturbd oceans . . .
A vague breath moves the wandering spheres
But no spirit exists in those immensities.

"Looking for the eye of God, I saw only a socket,
Vast, black, and bottomless, from whence the Night that dwells there
Streams out over the world and ever deepens;

"A strange rainbow encircles this somber pit,
Threshold of the old chaos whose shadow is nothingness,
Spiral engulfing the Worlds and Days!"

III

"Immovable Fate, mute sentinel,
Cold Necessity! . . . Chance, who, advancing
Among the dead worlds under the eternal snow,
Chills by degrees the paling universe,

"Do you know what you are doing, primordial power,
With your extinguisht suns, falling upon one another . . .
Are you sure of transmitting an immortal breath
Between a world that dies and another being born again? . . .

"O my father! is it thee that I sense in myself?
Hast thou the power to live and to conquer death?
Wilt thou have succumbd under the last effort

"Of that angel of nights whom the anathema struck? . . .
For I sense myself alone in my weeping and suffering,
Alas! and, if I die, everything is going to die!"

IV

No one heard the eternal victim groan,
Giving up to the world in vain all his pourd-out heart;
But, ready to faint and reeling without strength,
He calld upon the *one alone* — awake in Jerusalem:

"Judas!" he cried to him: "You know how they value me,
Make haste and sell me, and finish this haggling:
I am suffering, Friend! beaten to the ground.
Come! O you who, at least, have the strength of crime!"

But Judas went his way, discontent and brooding,
Finding himself badly paid, full of a remorse so alive
That he read his black deeds written on every wall . . .

At last, Pilate alone, who kept vigil for Caesar,
Feeling some pity, turnd by chance:
"Go look for this madman!" he commanded his satellites.

       V

It was him all right, this madman, this sublime insensate . . .
This forgotten Icarus climbing the skies again,
This Phaethon destroyd under the divine thunderbolt,
This beautiful murderd Atys whom Kybele reanimates!

The augur examined the side-wound of the victim,
The earth became drunk with that precious blood . . .
The stunnd universe reeld upon its axles,
And Olympus for an instant staggerd toward the Abyss.

"Answer!" cried Caesar to Jupiter Ammon:
"Who is this new god that is imposed on the earth?
And if this be not a god, it is at least a daemon . . ."

But the oracle invoked had to be forever silent;
One alone could explain this mystery to the world:
— He who gave soul to the children of the clay.

GOLDEN LINES

What!   Everything is sentient!
            —Pythagoras

Man, free thinker! do you believe yourself the one alone thinking
In this world where life bursts forth in everything?
Your free will disposes of the forces that you hold
But in all your councils the universe is absent.

Respect in the animal an active intellect:
Each flower is a soul in Nature bloomd forth;
A mystery of love lies conceald in the metal;
"Everything is sentient!"
            Everything has power over your being.

Beware in the blind wall a gaze that watches you:
To matter itself a voice is in-bound . . .
Do not make it serve some impious use!

Often in the obscure being dwells a hidden God;
And like a nascent eye coverd by its lids
A pure spirit grows beneath the skin of stones.

EARTH'S WINTER SONG

1

The beautiful young men and women!
Standing against the war their courage
has made a green place in my heart.

In the dark and utter destitution of winter
the face of the girl is a fresh moon
radiant with the Truth she loves,
the Annunciation, the promise
faith keeps in life.

Seed in the blind Earth, strikn by cold,
the spirits of the new Sun seek you out!

The face of Mary is a Star raying out.
And at the brest of her breth
"the Sun-element, the Child,
"forming Itself out of the clouds which have
"the Sun-rays in the atmosphere

"pouring thru them."

2

In the great storm of feer and rage
the heds of evil appeer and disappeer,
heds of state, lords of the cold war,
the old dragon whose scales are corpses of men
and whose breth blasts crops and burns villages
demands again his hecatomb,
our lives and outrage going up into his powr
over us.   Wearing the unctuous mask of Johnson,
from his ass-hole emerging the hed of Humphrey,
he bellows and begins over Asia and America
the slaughter of the innocents and the reign of wrath.

But our lives are drivn downwards too, within, deep down.
The spirits of the living stars return where the Sun
underground works his light magic
stirring the deepest roots.   We have been drivn
deep into the heart of our yearning, into the store
from which youth will rise, new shoots
of the spring-tide.   O the green spring-tide
of individual volition for the communal good,
the Christ-promise of brotherhood, the lover's
promise of the self's fulfillment!
"The body of inner Earth is alive in mid-Winter"

In the Under Ground:
the sublime Crèche - the lamp's faint glow,
the enormous shadows - the few
frightend shepherds - the three
magi or magicians seeing in the Child
the child of their lore - Joseph
whose faith is father, and the girl
whose virginity engenders - and the new
lord of the true life, of Love   •

we remember, was always born,
as now, in a time of despair,
having no place there at the Inn,
hunted down by Herod's law,
fleeing by night, secreted in Egypt.

Love in His young innocence
radiant in His depth of time and night
has waited and now—this is
the message of Christmas—returns once more,
bearing the light of the Sun
fair in His face.

MOIRA'S CATHEDRAL

*"The imaginary numbers," wrote Gottfried Wilhelm von
Leibnitz in 1702, "are a wonderful flight of God's Spirit; they
are almost an amphibian between being and not being."*

A field is "orderd" if the sizes of its
elements can be compared.

The sizes of its elements cannot
be compared.   For in the Eye of the Creator

the trembling of a leaf
in the roar of gun-fire,

the fall of a tree,   strikes dismay.

A thousand men go into the dirt and flood to die
having nor name nor proportion
in their numbers.   We

lose count.   An army—

a single man rising
rememberd   falling back
—I do not know who he is—
—where he is—
cries out.

Is it $17 million a day, a
million men finally to be laid down
in wager?

There is no Limit.

The hydra breaks from his confines
into Day's palaces

as many heads as he wants

(he moves the living bodies of men
forward
to fill the gap   •)

95

to win.　　Destroying

fields of rice, villages, bridges,
　　factories, defenses . . .

At the Grand Poker Table,
burning heads of their stogies
　　illustrating the battlefields,

eyes of that entity　　counting

　　on the play

　　his hands

shuffling the cards, beyond number.

A SHRINE TO AMEINIAS

Parmenides' Dream

Horses, cabalos cabbalas, that
    carry my thought up into those airy
    passages the heart desires and mind
leaps to search whose illusive boundaries
        cloud chamber bells of shifting
        resonance and tones

Iris in her chromatic scales
    out of Light / raises
      from teardrops   her violet
and red   outer limits of our
       sight
                weeping,

irradiate with self-defining
    steps of color into higher and lower
       realms set

among clouds where this chariot
    arrives, the brassy doors of day
       and night stand •

neigh and stamp their feet
    impatiently
—the axle blazing in the socket—
—the great wheels roaring round
       at each end, making
    the holes in the naves sing.   Now

the way of the Goddess opens,
and the Sun's daughters
    break thru night's sweet silences
first breaths and lights of their

        laughter from that orient horizon
        fading the stars' tinctures.

✦

Beyond the heart's reaches
Where the way goes

    fitted above with stone lintel
    and below, threshold of stone,

    the gates high in the air
    closed by great doors, as at Mykenai

to Parmenides Δικη Right Reason,

    armd, appeard, and would bar the way,
    under Whose retributive lock and key—

But his attendants,
bemusing Her with soothing words

    thus Avenging Justice changing
    to Mistress of the Unspoken Wish

and by craft persuading Her to undo

    that which She guarded,
    the weighty doors flung back,

straight thru the radiant maidens
led the horses and the car,

    space turning upon its brazen hinges
    to open wide / and deep dream

leading into light, the Lady

    spake to me, taking my hand in Hers,
    and said:
                Well come, youth,
    that comest to my house in this car

    drawn by such horses in truth and
    tended by immortal charioteers.

It is not by Chance, but Right and divine Justice
have sent you to travel this way.   Far indeed

  is this place from the minds of most men.

✤

Truth, She told Parmenides, was a well-rounded ring,
a circling without disturbance, seeming to move, but
having an unwobbling pivot, an unmoved heart—ατρεμης
is the Greek word: an untrembling center.
Yes, it is there, at the heart of the work, and
even in dreams, the world seems to encircle him,
sure in him. —And you've to learn too,
She promises, opinions in which there is no
true belief at all, the accounts of mortal men
(the word here is βροτός—βρότος, *the blood*
that has run from a wound).   Here, Truth trembles,
and you will learn how all things that seem,
as they pass thru all things, must take on
semblance of Being.   Immortal mortalities!

   Parmenides of Elea, shadowy being!
They said you were handsome; they said you were rich;
and that you followd the Pythagorean tramp Ameinias,
leaving Xenophanes, your teacher,
who had fame, for this man of whom we know only
this thing.   Love, certain as a well-rounded ring
made you sure in him.   Love, trembling, unsure,
seeming at times to have only the semblance of being,
sustain you.

Now there comes such a seeing: how
all things are present to the mind!   for it will not
sever What Is from Its belonging to What Is,
whether it be scatterd thruout space in time, or—
Grand Collage—brought together in this place we are.

          Once more,
Immortal Parmenides, I see you bereaved
in the death of your lover.   I see you in your dream
once more riding that car with its fiery horses,
desirous of high heaven's court, and the Sun's daughters

99

come to your aid.   Once more, the Great Goddess
speaks to you of the Way of Seeming, of Loss and the Blood
that has run from the Wound, and of
the Way of Truth.   "First," you tell us, "of all the Gods,
She created Eros."
                        Once more, remembering,
you build the shrine to Ameinias.

NARRATIVE BRIDGES FOR *ADAM'S WAY*

as presented in concert-reading version
February 4th & 11th, 1966
at the University of British Columbia, Vancouver

[Page references are to the text of the play as given in *Roots and Branches* (Charles Scribner's Sons, 1964), pages 127 thru 163]

NARRATOR

[preceding Adam's speech as prologos, page 127]

We have no agency today outside of a group of willing readers, would-be actors robbd of their action, bent out of sorts toward poetry, with these music-stands and chairs for their scene, and must beg of you to join us in all your good will and imagination to give the play time, place, scene, voice, as well as hearing.

We must return to the first power of words to call up scenes, at a stage before there was a stage, of worlds that we do not know ever were, and move out of phantoms of the mind half persons, half ideas, giving them what life they may have in being enacted. Should we darken the light of the stage until in that gloom, crawling, or shall it be slowly, painfully, walking? thru time, thru ages of time, our dragons come forward? Or let them come up from where they are, with no illusion of light and dark, chiaroscuro of the ingenious stage manager, but having only the darkening and lighting of your own (our own) picturing of them in your (our) mind's hearing their voices to give proper environs.

Tonight, no theater of illusions cast before your eyes, but all depending upon your own magic of active delusion, before eyes that ears call up in giving us audience, with words alone to incite the glitter of wet scales over the lizard back, the cold exciting air about to be a wet cloud, the maze of their own magic in which these—Hermes and Lilith—wind thru time and delusions of space, coming close upon a certain wood and a clearing therein, suspended in a time before the beginnings of first human things.

Here Erda-Urda, a sylph first, of the same order as Ariel in *The Tempest*, but drawn down then into the anguish of human being thru love's awakening, and two others, men of an elfin or fairy world, shadows of the earth cast upon the mirror of a cloud, or some mirage of being, cooperating between the seer's fatigue and an *ignis fatuus* of the sayer's argument, or are they pictures appearing in the air, cousins of the rainbow and the daydream? — dance. The two worlds coming together, Atlantis and the Dark Wood, converge upon the dreams of Adam unborn.

He speaks before the play:

✦ FIRST EXIT

[following Lilith's soliloquy *"The Moon is a great seed . . ."* and preceding Erda's soliloquy *"There is a chapel in the wood I know of . . ."*, page 135]

But now those great shadows and those dancing beams of the forest's light have gone back into themselves. We see not dragons and elves but shinings and shades of leafy solitudes, avenues leading back and back into depths of this world of trees. Erda coming forth alone addresses us:

✦ SETTING THE SEANCE SCENE

[following Erda's soliloquy, page 136, and preceding the seance scene, page 137]

A seance table has been set up and by the light of her spirit-lamp Mrs Maybe and Colonel Perkins, who may remind us of Madame Blavatsky and Colonel Olcott for the moment, sit as she lays out the Tarots or *Tarots* as she calls them after her author's habitual mispronunciation. But these are a deck strange to us. It is a table the imagination keeps between two worlds, and Mrs Maybe herself is that Moonmère of whom we have already heard in the play and her medium's cabinet is the Pod of Man in which the first human likeness grows and his twin-angel with him alike as two peas in a pod. When Adam is at last released into his own (our own), the archangel Samael too is released into his *great* form. And here we learn he is the Adversary, twin now not to Adam but to Michael, the Advocate.

> Mrs Webb and Mr Webb arrive (our dragons) a little late
> to take their place as the table begins to rock
> and Mrs Maybe's boy-medium begins to talk,
> and soon the balking of the play will break.

Then whatever semblance this little scene had of the actual world, of some theosophical roundtable in a London backroom in the 1880s, will fade and its actors step forward into the high impersonations they were meant for in the Irreal: Mrs Maybe (Dame Nature Herself), Colonel Perkins (the archangel Michael), Mr Webb (the demon Hermes), and Mrs Webb (the demon Lilith).

✦ THE POD OF ADAM

[following Mrs Maybe's "*You block my way!*" and preceding the entrance of Erda, Pook and Bobbin, page 140]

From the other side the fairies come, drawn to the Cabinet that in the Astral World is a great green Pod, ripening upon a stem from the other side, Earth-side, that those at the seance table call their line of contact. This vine has been portrayd in all the ancient tombs and temples, the vine whose grapes gave forth that wine that Noah drank and drew him down into a drunkenness of knowing, that vine whose roses twined to make a maze about the secret heart the would-be lover must penetrate and to amaze the mind, that vine whose pods are the animal wombs in time. Indeed, we are always so bemused, amused, wherever we come near thereto we know not for sure if it be grape-vine, rose-vine, bean-vine or the green ivy twines so between twins the cord between a mothering world and its dreaming infant worlds within.

Think of our own life-lines or life-times as being such a

vegetable thing, abundantly flowering and putting forth seed-pods of what we are, so that moments ripen and fall to earth, bursting with new plantings of ourselves in us—and these, subject to mutations, radioactive alterations and misunderstandings of our original form, puns, cross-messages of the first code we come from—and so we go to birth, to the leaping aliveness of a new beginning from the inertia of the blind wanderings of the plant we are in our going to seed.

But let me digress. For this idea of such a vine with its tendrils of feeling (but these are also tenderings of thought feeling their way, taking over the world of trees, climbing among whose branches) . . . Our lives grow, it is said, upon a trellis *"where the grape vine, the pampre, unites with the rose"* —the frame of Nature or of Divine Will—and at its tips the vine extends toward the light, curling to grip the fundamental intent, the sustaining form, but seeking too the rays of the sun toward new life. It is both blind and seeking then, our vine. Its seeds are eyes, and its lives visions enclosed therein. Each tip of green search in touch is an organ of sight, a secret eye.

Adam grows inside the Pod that swells upon Dame Nature's vine like a sleeping eye, a spirit hidden beneath closed lids of sleep that sends from the embryonic brain stems of sight into the depths of vision where eyes form in the skin between the Irreal and the Actual Real.

He has a kind of sight then of Pook and Bobbin who come with Erda to confront the womb in which he grows.

✴ TEARING DOWN THE WALLS

[following Bobbin's words, *"Tear the walls of this magic down / before his sleep ripens and he wakes a king"*; replacing stage directions at the top of page 143]

The fairies rip open the hanging pod, tearing down the walls of the medium's cabinet in this world, so that where a membrane was there is now a passage-way, a gap in the weave of things, revealing Adam, who falls out, inert as a doll. He lies upon the flowery bank of Eden, leaving a hole where he had been, where "God does rush in," as Olson once warnd me: "And art is washt away, turnd into that second force, religion." It is like a giving way of a wall of work that otherwise had held a sea at bay. Adam has withdrawn himself where he should have held his ground. Now he is fated to awake into our beginnings.

But, ripping open the womb of Man untimely, these elemental mid-wives or wiverns—the elves or dragons—have released more than Adam, for, where he falls, his angelic adversary, motionless as if unseen, stands: Samael, in whose fall Man first stood in jeopardy. But that was another play. From every knot we thought twinnd in the jeu d'esprit there are ties that bind more nets in numbers than we know to count.

Pook and Bobbin tear down the cabinet, revealing the Adam, who falls asleep, and in his sleep Samael stands watching. Pook stares into Adam's face to see if there are signs of life. Bobbin listens at his chest . . .

✢ THE FATE-SAYERS

[following Bobbin's "*Man's but a doll and all that / fearful restless thought is done,*" page 143]

Now from their places, Mrs Maybe, Colonel Perkins, advance, and the figure standing where the cabinet was joins them. These three come over to Eden-side where Adam lies, and, as Nature and the two archangelic powers, the dextrous hand and the sinister, they cast his fate.

✢ DISMISSAL OF THE FATE-SAYERS

[following the fate-casting scene and preceding Adam's soliloquy, page 144]

Return to your places, O spinners and weavers and cutters of our thread, upon whose spindles, spools, wheels, looms and scissors our plot is fashiond, our faces deepend, and our fates depend. Haven't you heard what's yours of us is not what's really ours of you? We but grow stronger in our selves as you would draw the strand of us thin and wear it out to all that adversity in which we have a pathetic role to play, and when the fabric breaks, in moods of emptiness or in madness, raving wild in the wood or on the mountain top, destitute of all our worldly goods and sense, we may look up to claim an unworldly good, no earthly good to us, cry "Love, Love, Love", having no answer, in solitude derive a tune and out of tune take heart, the lilt of some grievous air uplifting us or, *idée fixe* of color, red on red, the beat from word to word of a complaint, complaining, taking on the urgency of the sound of things, raising palaces and thrones,— and be a king of it, for all of it, lord it over nothing but its going on, and gain th'audience of no one we know exactly or certainly to advance our cause.

For Adam does not need your applause nor heed your ear's request in his speech but has only to speak to make his ways yours by, no other way, needs your patience patience patience then to bear with him, to be his, needs only the light of eyes that heed the way he's to go to be yours to see his way by.

✦ ADAM'S AWAKENING INTO THE PLAY

[following Adam's soliloquy and preceding Hermes' words *"What is the meaning of this . . ."*, page 146]

For the moment, he breaks from the confines of his part into his part again and almost speaks. Does god attend him? Where you attend him, you'll see certain secrets of the play—but he lapses (the secrets lapse) into that deep slumber in which his author intends to fashion all that old story of Lilith, first wife, the woman before Man was, mother of no one, and Eve, second wife, the woman after Man, in whom we are human, mother of us all then, and of Eden (is it dream or memory? homeland of the pleasure principle in the libidinal sea, an island girt round with forbidding walls?) and of the Serpent, the hydra Wisdom in the Tree of Knowledge of Good and Evil, that multiplies, rising until his snakey heads brood in all the lights and centers of our being, and to work certain sleights of hand and meaning therein.

For he comes about not from the creative power but from the creative need, from the creation of a manifest failure in God to love, in which the love that must be is first admitted. And God is like a wrathful stone struck with a fear and freezing in Itself with a wild anxiety, heart beat and heart ache at once awakening in Him, extending the rhythm in which the universe we know is created from His unknowing, and strikes out to inflict upon His creation the pangs in which His own heart labors. When Adam awakes from the travail of God's sleep, he will be the healing of the Creator from His creation He was meant to be. Grand and pitiable project! how I suffer in your sufferance, how I rage in your raging, how I fail in your faltering . . .

Were it not for this recurrence of the idea, Man, we would not imagine that the great Imaginer seeks His own self and knows not what It is but only that It's hidden in what fails, what falls from Him, what fouls the light in knowing with heat and drives the Holy Spirit Itself into Form and stories into Story to be undone. It is only to say that He will not know who He is until *we* know; He'll know nothing of seeing until *we* see. O, He is all we know of war, for we are no more than He *contends* we are. But He has also just that hope of freedom from what He is He has in us we feel as a yearning to pass beyond His conditions. He'll have no peace, for He has no peace in Him, until *we* make peace; no Love until we *make* Love, that now is no more than the regret or lure of a broken promise in us or a persistent wish.

✦ LILITH'S INCANTATION

[following Lilith's "*The ancient War is still in him*", replacing stage directions, page 149]

There is a falling down of the light thruout the world, and in the seance room Mrs Maybe's lamp goes out, until, as Lilith begins the words "*Night and her powers*", we are in the thrall of a total darkness.

[following Lilith's words *"but hint of what God's first Emptiness is"*, page 150]

She passes now into the region where Adam lies, standing at his boundary, to evoke from him God's void. Perhaps, before the betrayal of the Creator's secrets, Adam was no more than a reflection of his maker, having within no inkling of depths or distances. But now, toucht by the dragon's cold, the lingering knowledge of old orders in their extinction, he must reflect himself upon that which he is a reflection of. Creature of the creative angst, he is drawn into the magic of (the anxiety of), the creation of—his Self.

❧

[following Lilith's evocation-invocation of *"the Void He Is"*, and preceding the question and answer scene between Lilith and Adam, page 150]

In the inertia of nightmare, all-but-unbearable silences open between questioner and answerer. He asks, but she is the questioner. She answers, but he must know the answer. She means to so trouble him before life that all the divine instructions will be undone.

❧

[following Lilith's words *"You are dreaming . . ."*, page 151]

Slowly the dragon moves over him, keeping the nightmare pace of the scene, and covers him in the embrace of the incubus, awakening him with her kiss to her emptiness. After a long pause, she rises and begins to retreat, and her voice and her silences come now as echoes of what they were.

♣ ADAM'S AWAKENING IN EDEN

[following Lilith's words "Time's kisss . . .", and announcing the change to the Garden of Eden where Adam sleeps in the image of God, page 151]

But now we must raise the light, for when he wakes it is not to the Night of the Tomb, nor to the shifting glamors of the Astral Garden, but to the full light of Morning, of Eden-side. We see him upon some flowery bank in that deep slumber God the Father cast him into that He might bring forth from him the beginnings of the love that would create a woman. Erda, drawn from her airy spirit-world into Urda, earth-bound, comes to Adam's side, as if he cried out to her.

♣

[following Erda's words *"this one they call Moon or Man / is a mood in me"* and preceding her words *"Can you hear?"*, page 152]

She bends over the sleeping Adam. He seems half-pretend to her, as if he were a doll and the love that begins to stir a new nature were a play-love, and half-hope, as if he were the source he is to be, the end of girlhood's dreams and the fullness of womanhood's first reality.

♣

[following Michael's words *"From your base elements / you are removed and Day's your bride"*, and preceding Adam's waking, page 154]

He carries something of Night with him as he would wake, barely rising from its tides, opening his eyes as if in the thick of the wave that carries him, he talks to himself. But God's utter darkness, His emptiness that would fill itself in Creation, cannot illustrate itself, and Adam, whose way is knowing, must now make up what his Maker is and does not know. So, Satan finds that which he would summon to his side to undo Adam in

109

knowledge, a "Death" before the death known in the Tree of Good and Evil, a "Woman" and a "Kiss" before woman or kiss ever was. Satan-Samael is not that Nought or Nothing (Nihil, the "Night" before night was) but himself is one of the first Lights of Creation, Lucifer, Creation's idea of the threat of such a Nothingness from which It comes. And Michael must dismiss these ideas as contrary to the good of Creation, tho, did he ally himself with the whole of What Is, he would not raise the issue of choice in the tissue of things.

✤ THE TEMPTER

[following Samael's words "*and Adam must find himself in Eve*", page 158]

The angels leave, for this world is now to be for Eve and Adam alone. Oh yes, Samael must ever return to knock at their hearts or doors or drop his poison words in their unwary ears, but he can but draw his argument from a world that's theirs. It is he who listens everywhere, stoops to pick up and return what we would discard or forget. He over hears, we under stand not what he means in what he says.

✤

[following Eve's words "*and spoke again of our Author's delite / in various Truth*", page 159]

Adam steps forward and addresses the world in soliloquy, leaving Eve alone. He is like a poet entering his art, where "*In the beginning was the Word*" has a peculiar meaning verging upon vanity, and in the childlike vain pleasure of the poet with his words, Adam would name the things of his world his.

Samael enters then, and, as if he were Eve's awareness that she has of the loneliness of named things, he hovers about Eve, unseen, but a presence, a voice felt or almost heard upon the air at her waiting ear.

✤

[following Samael's words *"It is the Tree of the Other Side,
of what is more"*, page 162]

Eve closes her eyes, and Samael kisses her, awakening in her
the grievous knowledge of the denial of Love in which he dwells
and, in that, of the risk of Love in which she lives.

✤ *CLOSE*

Eve   O Adam, something has happend, I know!
         I am ashamed.   O
         heal me with a kiss.

Narrator   She kisses him.   *All of human wisdom
             seems to fall
       into the reawakend depth of mystery.*
            She but touches on
       a fear from which he came originally.

       The stage (our world) is plunged into dark
            Lights out!

       They cling to the shaking acknowledgment of their love,
       like children hugging a spar the wave flings high,
       and fall into that Night men call despair
       when all is lost or left behind.   Then Nature
       enters with Her lamp, Good Nurse of what is Hers,

       and quickens their night-time with Her glow.

111

From the body-remains of the bull Hadhayans
the food!   the immortality of the people!

"No-man's land in which everything moving
—from Saigon's viewpoint—was 'hostile' "

They've to take their souls in the war

as the followers of Orpheus   take soul in the poem

the wood to take fire from that dirty flame!

in the slaughter of man's hope

distil the divine potion,   forbidden hallucínogen

that stirs sight of the hidden

order of orders!

They've to go into the war   and have no other

scene to make   time to live   •

Dieu,   dont l'oeuvre va plus loin que notre rêve

Creator   mysterious Abyss

from which there goes out a smoke
of men, of beings, and of suns!

so deep that he is blue with depth

containing without deception   what so deceives us.

The extent of the shadow   the weight of the fullness

measure

parts of a sentence   they must make their long march to make

life writes   we take as necessity.

And in order to liberate the New China
from Chiang Kai-shek, Presbyterian warlord, his bankers
　　raiding the national treasury, his armies
　　paid with bribes (aid) from Roosevelt and Stalin,
　　against Mao, exterminating cities,

Mao's own mountain of murderd men,

　the alliteration of ems like Viet Nam's

　　　　burnd villages . . .

　(Johnson now, no inspired poet but making it badly,
　　　amassing his own history in murder and sacrifice

　　without talent)

　　. . . irreplaceable　　irrevócable　　in whose name?

　　　a hatred the maimd and bereft must hold

against the bloody verse America writes over Asia

　we must recall　　to hold　　by property rights that

　　are not private (individual) or public rights but

　　　given properties of our common humanity.

"The United States themselves are essentially the greatest poem"?

　Then America, the secret union of all states of Man,

　waits, hidden and challenging, in the hearts of the Viet Cong.

　"The Americans of all nations at any time upon the earth,"

　　Whitman says—the libertarians of the spirit, the

　　　devotées of Man's commonality.

"To unite ourselves with you we have renounced
All creatures of prey: False gods and men"

　　l'oeuvre qui va plus loin que notre rêve

　Solidarius : solderd　　this army having its sodality

113

in the common life,   bearing the coin or paid in the coin
solidum, gold emblem of the Sun

    tho we fight underground

from the heart's volition,   the body's inward sun,

    the blood's natural

    uprising   against tyranny   •

And from the first it has been communism,   the true

    Poverty of the Spirituals   the heart desired;

    I too removed therefrom by habit.

    ❦

They fight the invader

or cower, fear so striking them, unmannd by hunger or having

no dream of manhood,   the Sun

    does not last in them;

or conscripted, the pay being no goal, they are not true soldiers,

    not even sold on the war

but from fear of punishment go, compelld, having no

    wish to fulfill in fighting

but killing, killing,   to be done with it.

O you, who know nothing of the great theme of War,
fighting because you have to, blindly, at no frontier
    of the Truth but in-
structed by liars and masters of the Lie, your own
    liberty of action
    their first victim,

youth, driven from your beds of first love and
    your tables of study to die

in order that "free men everywhere" "have the right
    to shape their own destiny
in free elections"— in Las Vegas, in Wall Street,
    America turns in the throws of "free enterprise",
    fevers and panics of greed and fear.

The monstrous factories thrive upon the markets of the war,
and, as never before, the workers in armaments, poisond
    gasses and engines of destruction, ride
high on the wave of wages and benefits. Over all,
the monopolists of labor and the masters of the swollen
    ladders of interest and profit survive.

    The first Evil is that which has power over you.

      Coercion, this is Ahriman.

    In the endless Dark   the T. V. screen,
    the lying speech and pictures   selling its time and produce,
corpses of its victims burnd black by napalm

    —Ahriman, the inner need for the salesman's pitch—

the image of the mannequin, smoking, driving its car at high speed,
elegantly dresst, perfumed, seducing, without

    odor of Man or odor of sanctity,

in the place of the Imago Xristi;

      robot service in place of divine service;

  the Good Word and Work   subverted by the Advertiser,

    He-Who-Would-Avert-Our-Eyes-From-The-Truth.

    Habit, this is Ahriman.

    The first Evil is that which conscripts you,

spreading his "goods" over Asia.   He moves in, you let him

    move in, in your own interest, and it serves you right,

he serves you as you let him.   Glimmers of right mind

obscured in the fires   he scatters.

Master of Promises,   Grand Profiteer and Supplier!

the smoking fields, the B-52s flying so high   no sound   no sight
   of them gives warning,   the fliers dropping their bombs
having nor sight nor sound of what they are bombing.

This is Ahriman, the blind

destroyer of the farmer and his ox at their labor.

The Industrial wiping out the Neolithic!   Improver of Life

flying his high standards!

Who makes the pure into wicked men,
Who lays waste the pastures and takes up arms against the righteous.

July 1965-July 1966
October 1966

AN INTERLUDE

My heart beats to the feet of the first faithful,
    long ago dancing in Broceliande's forest,
And my mind when it ceases to contend with the
    lies and dreams of Generalissimo Franco
delites in the company of defeated but glorious men
    who have taken to the highlands or,
in love with the people, striven to keep secret ways
    of brotherhood and compassion alive,
      spreading Truth
like seeds of a forbidden hallucinogen, marijuana or morning glory
    hidden away among the grasses of the field.

Love long conceald!   Love long suffering!
Love we never knew   moved us from the beginning!
Now it may be we are driven to your high
    pasture.   Hard presst,
my heart opens as if there were a pass in the rock,
    unknown, a by-pass,
close enough to be very like death.

Solitary door, road of solitudes,
the mute song at last sung in the veins among strangers!
I must go to the old inn in the canyon beyond us,
to the roller-skating rink among the pine trees.

For the dancers have come down from the mountains,
and the piano player strikes up such a sound the fiddler
sails away in the waving and waist-clasping rounds of it.
The people, then, are the people of a summer's night over and gone,
the people of a Polish dance hall before the last war,
in the sweat and reek of Limburger cheese and Bermuda onions,
sweltering in beer and music, Kansas country evangels,
or summer people in the Catskills
who have taken up square-dancing   as the poet takes up
measures of an old intoxication that leads into poetry,
not "square" dancing, but moving figures,

the ages and various personae of an old drama . . .

coupling and released from coupling,
    moving and removing themselves, bowing
and escaping into new and yet old
    configurations,
the word "*old*" appearing and reappearing
    in the minds of the youths dancing

. . . so that I remember I was an ancient man in that
part of the dance, *Granpaw*, I was nineteen and yet ninety,
taking the hand of Little Nell, dolce-doeing,

and the dance, the grand seance of romancing feet in their numbers,
    forward and back—we were the medium
for Folk of the Old Days in their ever returning.

❖

In the great figure of many figures the four
    directions and empires
change into four times, and opposites of
    opposites meet and mate,
separating and joining, ascending a ladder of litanies
    until they are "sent"—
losing themselves in each other's being
    found again.

Now, because I am Fire and you are Water,
Water and Fire kiss and embrace.
Water and Fire dance together.   This,
    the grand mimesis,
imitates the wholeness we feel true to What Is.

❖

We must go back to sets of simple things,
hill and stream, woods and the sea beyond,
the time of day—dawn, noon, bright or clouded,
five o'clock in November five o'clock of the year—

changing definitions of the light.

And say the dancers take the six unbroken lines of the Chinese
    hexagram,
and six dance for the six broken lines, the six gates or openings
in the otherwise stable figure: there are twelve in all.
Dividing into groups of three, they dance in four groups.

What twelve things of your world will you appoint guardians,
      Truth's signators?
Salt, Cordelia said.   Gold and lead.
    The poet, the great maker of wars and states, and
the saint, Burckhardt named as the three creative
      masters of history.
But now, let the twelve be unnamed.

The dancers come forward to represent unclaimd things.

In the War they made a celestial cave.

In the War now I make

      a celestial cave,   a tent of the Night

(the Sun, no longer striking day upon the Earth,

but light-years away   a diamond spark in the host of stars
    sparkling net   bejewelld wave of dark   over us
  distant coruscations
                "play of light or of intellectual brilliancy"

in which I pretend   a convocation of powers

(under the cloak of his poem   *he* retires

      invisible

           so that it seems no man   but a world speaks

for my thoughts are servants of the stars, and my words

     (all parentheses opening into

    come from a mouth that is the Universe   *la bouche d'ombre*

    (The poet-magician Dr Dee in his black mirror
     calls forth his spirits from their obscurity)

thru the rays of invisible and visible bodies,

      known and unknown   sources and senders,

thru fumes, lights, sounds, crystallizations . . .

For now in my mind all the young men of my time
   have withdrawn allegiance from *this world*, from public things .

   and as their studies in irreality deepen,

      industries, businesses, universities, armies

        shudder and cease

so that the stone that comes into being
when the pupil of the eye that like a moon
takes all seeing from an unseen sun's light
      reflected makes
held under his tongue each man speak
        wonders to come.

          Chaos / and the divine measures and orders

          so wedded are

          we have but to imagine

          ourselves the Lover

          and the Beloved appears

man and woman, child and king, the ages and ladders of being,
    the labor of birth and the release of death   so compounded therein

        they draw from the War Itself withdrawing

          this breath between them.

     In this rite the Great Magician stirs in His dream,

       and the magician dreaming   murmurs to his beloved:

          thou art so near to me
          thou art a phantom that the heart
            would see—

and now the great river of their feeling grows so wide

      its shores grow distant and unreal.

now down-falling doom's darling,
    one feather of his wing / lost

    in God's gaze   found   *Libertas*

the Master Victor Hugo saw in that dream
    Poetry is / or at his singing tables

    heard rumor of

an angelic being true to Lucifer
    as Satan was false to his Self / and fell,

    brooded in the roots of power as if

    it be his own,

divorced from that Love, light *and* dark,
    source of all   ˈ.e call

        Wing of our Mothering Universe

        in whose image destroying and
          guardian angels are guerdond,

wingd lions / ladies, giant butterflies
in fields of suns, amongst galaxies

        given wings,

        sporting,

        Fancy descries.

From the trunk of whose gorgon-wild head flying up
Pegasos / that great horse Poetry,   Rider

        we ride, who make up

        the truth of What Is;

and, as if Eros unbound, AntEros / bound
free to love, Chrysaor / of the golden sword—

twins of that vision in which from the
old law's   terrible sentence

wingd   the new law springs

        •

    darkling

        •

        lumen

Cao-Daï

gold and crystal of the Sky's reaches!

First from the Father   glance that lit

New Love in Liberty   whose law

dissolves in its coruscations
(rainbow) (lapis lazuli)

the chains of Eros and the Old Law!

Christmas Eve, 1925.   The Spirit descended
to bring the Truth to Viet-Nam.

Réjouissez-vous de cette fête,

anniversary of my coming to the West
to give my Sign

that certain hearts tremble
and pour out from their reserves

enduring Love . . .

*Du haut de la tour sans toit où l'Extase m'a porté
j'ai regardé le monde triste et froid, noir et agité*

From the height of the endless tower where Ecstasy carried me:
I have gazed at the cold and sad world, black, and agitated . . .

*Du haut de la tour sans toit où la Foi m'a élevé:
j'ai vu la mer d'en haut   gardant la serenité bleue
d'une Vierge qui ne se dévoile . . .*

And the black opend up,   a god

in trouble came, like an eye   opening,
lids of the sorrow and the cold   trembling,

into a glance,   striking . . .

it was no more than a feather lost in the tumult

    turnd,   high in the up-wind

  he fell so far from her

               (as if a hand   sustaind me

          Day opend in the Abyss

his glance awakening   flames in the under ground

And the angels, shaking with love, regarded her.
The Xerubim, the great twins, who cleave one to the other,

    the legions of anger and the hosts of wrath,

the constellations of morning and of evening,
the Powers, the Intelligences, longd to see
this sister born of paradise and of hell

    l'Ange Liberté.

The visage of the Father undergoes changes in the thought of her,

  his rage falters, returns, falters . . .

in the chains of the First Eros, AntEros / longs to be free.

    ✢

From the height of the endless tower whereto Faith lifted me
  I have seen the sea from above
    guarding the blue serenity of a Virgin
    who does not reveal Herself.

Du haut de la tour sans toit où l'Espérance m'a conduit:
  j'ai vu l'étoile d'un matin sans soir et un jour infini—

I have seen the star of a morning without night and an infinite day.

          Whereto Love brought me:

  I gazed upon the source, my Lord the Sun,

    that illumines the Earth.

From the height of the tower that has no roof:
I have seen the ship of shadows cross the sea of light

/ and, beyond words,

I have contemplated the Regulator of the Stars,
                Commissar of Invisible and Visible Worlds.

   The President of the Grand Symphony

       for the sake of a dread calm and harmony

sets into motion   a counter-point   of contending elements,

    music's   divine Strife.   At Montségur,

that the heart be tried,

Corba de Perella,
Ermengarde d'Ussat,
Guilleline, Bruna, Arssendis,

Guillaume de l'Isle,
Raymond de Marciliano,
Raymond-Guillaume de Tornaboïs,
Arnald Domerc,
Arnald Dominique . . .

these among the seventeen
receiving the *consolamentum* to join the two hundred and ten *perfecti*
at the field of the fiery martyrs, *Champs de Cramatchs*,
until the name of the Roman Church with its heapt honors
    stinks with the smell of their meat burning

enter as notes of a sublime sweetness
the resounding chords of wrath and woe.   Grandeur!

At the Saint-Siège Caodaïste   at Tay-Ninh,

    in the roaring din of American planes
    performing their daily missions to destroy
    the Viet-Cong's strongholds of the Holy Spirit

the prayers of the shaman-priests at the altar

      rise / and in the crescendo of the War,

exact the line of a melody / as if

    the faith of Schubert would enter the Heraklitean truth,

          the polemic

  father of all,   harsh necessity,

              in the roar and fire-fall,
     bear

this sonance,   his son

    and the Note to mount

          they sound

sentences of an inaudible bell.

"It's not so, not strictly so,
     that's the trouble,"   Ezra Pound, Venice
1964

Slowly the toiling images will rise,
Shake off, as if it were débris,
     the unnecessary pleasures of our lives
And all times and intents of peaceful men
Reduce to an interim, a passing play,
     between surpassing
Crises of war.

                    Upon the stage before:

He brings the camera in upon the gaping neck
     which now is an eye of bloody meat   glaring
     from the womb of whose pupil   sight

springs to see,   two   children of adversity.

The Mother's baleful glance in romance's
                              head of writhing snakes haird

          freezes the ground.

                         Okeanos   roars,

wild oceanic father,   visage   compounded of fury and of wind

     (the whole poem becoming a storm   in which faces arise)

          Mouths yawn immensely   and hours,
                         as if they were mad brothers,
stare.

               From the body of the poem, all that words create

presses forth to be: youth,   with lightning flash
   that now is sword of gold, two-edged,
                      or of sun-glare
  cutting eye-nerve,
            painful youth!

And Pegasos springs   "born near the *springs* of Ocean"

ὁτ Ωκεανου περι πηγας γενθ

He-who-spurts-up   from the broken arteries   carotids   out of

   deep sleep the blood carries   upward

            (Ocean then, the drowsy deep)

     awakend
         flies

  to Zeus-Father above,
               Lord of the Deep Skies, whose House
    awaits him,
          the pressure of whose tides
upon the shores of life is like a horse raging,
   thunderous hooves,   striking

     flashes of light from unbright matter.

In the carved panel of the sarcophagus from Golgoi
[The Metropolitan Museum of Art, *Handbook of
the Cesnola Collection of Antiquities from Cyprus.*
As given in Cook, *Zeus,* volume two, part one, page
718]

the twain   rise to form for this moment
  the head of a new monster

               Genius

so starts up, affrighted,   of sudden stroke

"the which a double nature has" (Spenser

telling his syllables here)

that from the Garden verse addresses   each word

> *"It sited was in fruitfull soyle of old,*
> *"And girt in with two walles on either side;*
> *"The one of yron, the other of bright gold,*
> *"That none might thorough breake, nor ouer-stride:*
> *"And double gates it had, which opened wide"*

the wound become so wide a door

a deed

(the skull fragments and brain splatterd over the car's
upholstery,   the red of blood and roses mixing
in a flash)

(*"So foule and faire a day I have not seene,"* another
murderous heart declares, who from Medusa's head
expects that Burning Would—to echo Joyce's pun—
will never come to Dance Inane:

> *"Come, seeling Night,*
> *"Skarfe up the tender Eye of pitiful Day,"* he cries:
> *"And with thy bloodie and invisible Hand*
> *"Cancell and teare to pieces that great Bond,*
> *"Which keepes me pale.   Light thickens . . ."*

Shakespeare sees how in the assassin's mind
the world is filld with enemies,   the truth
itself is enemy and quickens   action to override
subversive thought.

> *"Ile fight,"* Macbeth declares: *"Give me my Armor."*
>
> *"Tis not needed yet."*
>
>   *"Ile put it on:*
> *"Send out more Horses; skirre the Country round,*
> *"Hang those that talke of Feare . . ."*)

in which the nation's secreted
sum of evil is betrayd

        Dionysos, Zeus's Second Self,

          Director of the Drama,
          needed.

   ❖

Dark figures move, flares / scatter in the night.
And from the stage / wild hammerings, a frightful pulse
Begins. Behind the lids / an after-image burns
And the tortured spirit in the meat remembers now
The nation has gone so far in wrong / Truth grows fateful
And true song gives forth portents of woe.   Sublime

Forbidden intensities convert the personal,
          and from what *I* am
Masks of an old pageant, from my world and time
Portentous rimes, foreshadowings history become a plot demands.
        The dramatist
Would not misunderstand the *melos* "romantic and sensational,
    with both song and instrumental music interspersed"
Taking over the place of the Real, dims humanity and moves us
          toward its own End.   *Melodramatic*

His language, and from his troubled mind
Echoes of speeches, incantations, wild prayers,
As if to teach us "the perfection of certain ideals,
    the depravity of others", he casts upon the wind.

        (The President
         orders history
         reupholsterd)

Upon the sarcophagus of we know not whom,
each figure, impending, become a sign,

Perseus with the head in a wallet
turns his back and marches off
("to be followd by his hound," the scholar observes
—exactly the figure of Le Mat in the
Ancien Tarot de Marseilles—"hounded" then).
Another figure gives Perseus wingd cap,
sandals and caduceus of Hermes: Macbeth
so little knows he moves as
messenger of the myth, the
  plot of the play.

And from the dying body of America I see,
or from my dying body,

       emerge

 children of a deed long before this deed,
 seed of Poseidon, depth in which the blue above
 is reflected

     released

huge Chrysaor and Pegasos sword and flash

   Father of Geryon, of him
    who carries Dante and Virgil into Hell's depths,

   and Steed of Bellerophon

    beneath whose hooves once again
    new springs are loosed on Helicon.

GOD-SPELL

        We have lost.   No,
    we have not lost   our way

      but we have found the way

  dark, hard to make out,   and yet
    joyous.

          What we hold to is no more than
    words.   Yes, it is hard to assay

    the worth we hold to.

       We said it was gold.   The soul

   weighd against Maat's feather.

Our treasure, the light in the dandylion head shining,
    they wld blow out.   "See, your heart holds to
    a lost cause."

            The light all but invisible

  seeds   scatterd abroad,   rise

    fall   upon the breath of the air

      everywhere   and in heavy ground

 find refuge.   This

the song of the *dent de lion* or of the thistledown

      seeds of a rumor   from hearts long ago

   defeated faiths   blown out

      the ayre of the music   carries.

EPILOGOS

and as an old man come forward
into a speech he had long waited for . . .

I have grown from a wrathful bough of the tree.
When I say *Love* the word comes out of me
like a moan—life-sap.   From broken wood.
Yet I would not have it come easily.
The word, the truth and the light of it
are one I have not won in myself.
Yes, how many times I have broken word
with you, generously, broken my word,
with you generously understanding me
I cannot understand.   It's all but words,
and men have said that too many times it seems.
I do not know in what I am myself.   True,
untrue, to that speaking with these things,
sounds and compounds of sounds men define
and pronounce differently riming—how is one
to speak making speech with such utterings?
Sometimes I think all that I call my life
is a placing, a place in the wood of that tree
the universe would face—force—to come green,
make a way, and I am—what a man is—
is no more than a blind—but it's pent up—
forcing out of us a statement, a green bud,
where creation that's a tree
must speak as it can to make
figures of man-kind, word-speakers,
in what it cannot see.

Again:

I return to you to see how near
you are to me, dear certainty in which I
    risk

certain uncertainties.   There must be for you
    too—
I see in your eyes your sight of me
—for you too, times
when all that we are bound to feel
bounds with life, leaps up,
and your eyes shine in the shining of
    my seeing you.   Brimfull
the cup my heart is upon the very
    edge
of spilling its more than can be contain, its
    happening so
in what is happening, deepens
    and fills with the
fact of your being, takes all that it can gather
    of that immanence
until the depths of the trembling water . . .
    (or is the soul,
ever so returnd to this wedding at Cana,
    toucht and re-turnd,
wine? Amethyst, blood-red ruby
    the color of the life of me I've to offer
up to Death's lips, for now I see

He drinks the full flood of grief and joy,
    the full flood of me, down
and breaks the empty cup upon the sill.
    He honors what I was
I am)   shines with the light you are
    for me.

    Again:

There it is.   You can depend on it.
The speech comes back to where it left off
in me.   A tree, a cup,
cannot contain themselves for a feeling that
returns in whatever it can—a river,

135

a single star,
a bird I cannot see sings—
and I would rehearse the sounds of the names of
    everything
to release this old necessity and shake
    with its need.

I think I was talking of talking and
    saying
my words cannot persuade you to or let me,
for you are listening, and charm moves
from a dumb ache I know.

Go aside from what matters. Have a
walk about. Take my stand / and
the pressure of morning grows in my chest
a chain of emotions lockt in one *mo* . . one . . .
the rime wont come thru or I wont
accept the word "*moan*". This is not—
I wouldnt own up to the truth of it
—mine. Man himself moand in me.
Opening my eyes

    everything I see / glows or shines.
Enrich with paintings, books, growing plants,
the room, the mind, the fund
I draw on, contains such a word:
the tree, the cup, the star, the bird
in all the rich garden of what we would cultivate in ourselves
moan   and strive to utter what they are
up.
        "Were you looking over my shoulder
when I was reading Keats
last night?

                    '. . . *wrung*
    By sweet enforcement and remembrance dear . . .' "

Your testimony enters here, his words:

136

'. . . So let me be thy choir, and make a moan
Upon the midnight hours . . .'

To husband so or wive the intimate
    happenstance in which our
continuity returns I'll
    take whatever words for it that fit
—Keats the key to unlock
love's moan from my unwilling lips.

   Again:

But now my will goes where Love I have
    spoken of 's
released.   I am a man of words, a
man of my word.   I get the drift I do not
know.   The Word moves me.   I give in to it.
I give into it my will, into it
the intent of the poem.   Death I see
that way, my Life is His.   He
has His will of me.   My Death!
unites me with the primary thought of you.
For I have filld my solitude with your being,
my essence dwells in your love
His will beyond belief the cup of a
    sorrowing night
in which the Sun rises that will rise
—in the shattering of the cup   He
    keeps the cup—

    shines, invisible,
having no style His speech so transparent
    is,   the Sun
in auroras of the wine in my
    solitude I have in you
        rises.

137

NOTES

(Where sources have not been given in the texts of the poems themselves, I list them below):

Bending the Bow: see G.S. Kirk, *Heraclitus, The Cosmic Fragments*, Fragment 51.

At the Loom, Passages 2: *Oxford English Dictionary*, volume XII, "Warp, sb".

As In The Old Days, Passages 8: Jacob John Sessler, *Communal Pietism Among Early American Moravians*.

The Architecture, Passages 9: Gustave Stickley, *Craftsman Homes* (1909)

Truman Michelson, *The Owl Sacred Pack of the Fox Indians*, Bulletin 72, Bureau of American Ethnology.

Wine, Passages 12: Baudelaire, *Du Vin et du Haschisch*. Rimbaud, "Enfance", *Illuminations*.

The Fire, Passages 13: Ficino, letter to Antonio Canisiano, quoted in D.P. Walker, *Spiritual and Demonic Magic from Ficino to Campanella*.

Whitman, *The Eighteenth Presidency*.

Chords, Passages 14: see W.K.C. Guthrie, *Orpheus and the Greek Religion* (second edition, 1952).

Spelling, Passages 15: Jespersen, Part I: "Sounds and Spellings", *A Modern English Grammar on Historical Principles*. See particularly 2.428.

Liddell & Scott, *Greek-English Lexicon* (eighth edition, 1897) article on *chi*.

O.E.D., volume I, "Ache, Ake".

Currents, Passages 16: Address to Mandoulis, quoted by Festugière, *La Révélation d'Hermès Trismégiste*, I: "La Vision de Dieu".

Moving the Moving Image, Passages 17: version of "The Perfect Sermon or The Asclepius", see G.R.S. Mead, *Thrice Greatest Hermes*.

The Torso, Passages 18: Marlowe, *Edward II*.

An Illustration, Structure of Rime XXVI, Passages 20: Maeterlinck, *The Blue Bird*. The poem illustrates a collage by Jess now in the collection of Kenneth Anger.

In The Place Of A Passage 22: Victor Hugo, "Pleine Mer", *La Légende des Siècles*.

Orders, Passages 23: Proclus, *Commentaries on Plato's Timaeus*, translated and annotated by Thomas Taylor.

Earth's Winter Song: Rudolf Steiner, *The Four Seasons and the Archangels*.

Moira's Cathedral: Philip J. Davis, "Number", *Scientific American*, September 1964.

A Shrine to Ameinias: see Kirk and Raven, *The PreSocratic Philosophers*.

The Soldiers, Passages 26: *The Hymns of Zarathustra*, Jacques Duchesne-Guillemin, translated by Mrs. M. Henning.

Victor Hugo, *La Légende des Siècles*, LIX.

Eye of God, Passages 29:

Gabriel Gobron, *Histoire et philosophie du Caodaïsme*.

Zoé Oldenbourg, *Massacre at Montségur*.

New Directions Paperbooks—A Partial Listing

For a complete listing request a free catalog from New Directions, 80 Eighth Avenue, New York, NY 10011; or visit our website, www.ndpublishing.com

†Bilingual

For a complete listing request a free catalog from New Directions, 80 Eighth Avenue
New York, NY 10011; or visit our website, www.ndpublishing.com

†Bilingual